The Ultimate
Wall Book

The Ultimate
Wall Book

VICTORIA ELLERTON

NORTH LIGHT BOOKS

Cincinnati, Ohio

To Angie and Rod for pointing me in the right direction

First published in Great Britain in 1998
by Collins & Brown Limited

First published in North America in 1998
by North Light Books
an imprint of F & W Publications, Inc.
1507 Dana Avenue
Cincinnati, OH 45207
1-800/289-0963

Library of Congress Cataloging-in-Publication Data:
A catalog record for this book
is available.

ISBN O-89134-928-6
1 3 5 7 9 8 6 4 2

Conceived, edited and designed by Collins & Brown Limited.
Editorial Director: Colin Ziegler
Art Director: Roger Bristow
Editor: Jinny Johnson
Designer: Sarah Davies
Assistant Editor: Claire Waite
Photographer: Lucinda Symons
Illustrator: Ian Sidaway

Reproduction by Hong Kong Graphic and Printing Ltd
Printed and bound in Hong Kong

Contents

Introduction

Walls are the backdrop of life. They can soothe or inspire, relax, or animate. The right design and decoration produces a surprising inner contentment – never underestimate the pleasure to be gained from a room you feel happy in.

In their simplest form, walls protect us from the elements and provide interior space in which to build our individual homes. At the other end of the spectrum, walls have surrounded and protected empires. They divide countries and cultures – the demolition of the Berlin Wall affected millions. Walls are powerful structures. They surround prisons, support skyscrapers, and dwarf people.

This book aims to inspire creativity and instill confidence, not to dictate. Two decades of wall decoration have left me open to individual tastes and changing fashions. I try my best to step into my clients' shoes, whether sneakers, brogues, boots, or stilettos, and it is the very diversity of their requirements and the infinite variety of decorative solutions that keep me swooshing the brush 20 years on. The different priorities in homes I have worked in have taught me that no rules are hard and fast. My visual sense is therefore relatively free from tradition and I relish the new and alternative.

In the style directory you will find a variety of ways to bring the walls in your home to life. Step-by-step illustrated directions bring even the most sophisticated techniques within easy reach of the enthusiastic amateur.

To apply more exciting and rewarding effects requires one simple thing – confidence. The transformed room will be an original and highly personal creation. Banish the sedate restrictions of tradition and unleash your feel for colour. Enjoy your walls!

Victoria Ellerton

Victoria Ellerton 1998

Assessing Your Walls

DECORATING OFTEN BEGINS with a long stare at blank walls. It is important to remember at this daunting stage that the colour and effect you choose is just to cover the 'shell' of the room. Curtains, pictures, rugs, furniture, and books will all divert the eye in the finished space. It is only in minimalist interiors that walls come under close scrutiny.

When decorating a small room with little natural light, most people choose pale colours in the hope of making the room appear bigger and lighter. In my experience this is a fallacy and such rooms look much better painted in deep, rich colours, which give them a cosy look. Naturally light and lofty rooms, on the other hand, do appear more spacious when decorated in light colours.

Look at the shape and proportions of your room. If the room is full of sloping alcoves and irregular corners, don't try an intricate geometric design or stripes. Choose a more forgiving treatment, such as colourwashing.

Warm elegance

Painted in rich earthy colours, this sitting room is extremely elegant, yet warm and welcoming. The darker red above the picture rail reduces the height and makes the room comfortable and intimate. Despite its strength, the red is soft and unthreatening with its browny tones. Another, equally bold, colour scheme can be glimpsed in the next room.

Looking at the room

BEFORE DECIDING ON A SCHEME for your room, think about how and when it will be used. Is it a daytime or evening room, or will it double as both? Deep, sumptuous colours are ideal in a room used mainly in the evening, but you might prefer lighter shades in a room you may be in all day. Is the room to be a private haven or used for entertaining? Will that entertaining usually be formal or more casual? Bright bold primaries encourage a fun, casual atmosphere. Neutral subtle shades might be more suitable for more conventional gatherings. Do you like to live among a clutter of books, magazines, and ornaments? Or do you like everything to have its place?

All these factors will influence your choice of wall treatment. Bear in mind that colours change in different rooms and locations. A warm creamy yellow that is the perfect solution for a south-facing room could seem mean and uninviting in a north-facing one. Blues always suit a sunny, south-facing room, but a blue in a north-facing room should be warmed with a touch of green to avoid an icy look. Walls painted in simple white emulsion/latex look wonderful in a room that has plenty of natural light, while rich reds and burnt terracottas are a cheering, warming influence in a room with little sun.

Finishing touches

Walls may be beautifully painted or papered, but they are only fully brought to life when furniture is positioned against them, and pictures and other objects are put in place. The right lighting is vital to the success of a room. Light from several low lamps is much softer and more welcoming than a central hanging light.

CHECKLIST

Below is a list of points to consider before starting to decorate your room

- Check the number of electrical points in a room. It is nearly always worth installing more than you think you might need and it is obviously better to do this before decorating.

- Have any really bumpy walls replastered and leave them to dry as long as possible before decorating.

- Complete any carpentry work in the room, such as book shelves before starting to decorate.

- Choose materials for curtains and upholstery at an early stage so that you can make sure the walls compliment them.

- Decide on flooring. Any sanding of floorboards should be done before decorating. Carpets should be fitted afterwards.

- Make sure you have enough paint, wallpaper, or tiles to complete the job – colours may vary in different batches.

- Work in the right order. Start by applying all the necessary coats to the ceiling. Then undercoat the walls and woodwork together. Complete the final coat on the walls first and then finish the woodwork.

Grounding the room

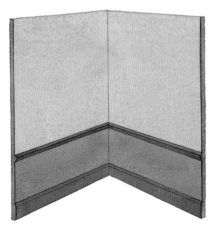

Painting the walls below the dado in a stronger colour than the area above makes the room seem better grounded and gives a feeling of solidity and strength.

Reducing the height

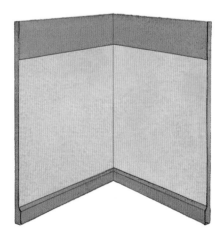

Using a stronger colour on the area above the picture rail than on the walls below reduces the feeling of height in a lofty room and makes the space seem cosier and more intimate.

Increasing the height

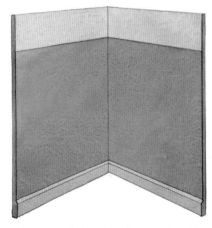

Painting the wall above the picture rail a lighter colour than the rest can make a low room seem taller and gives a feeling of extra space.

Wall dividers

ONE OF THE FEW RULES of successful decorating is to create proportions that lie easily with each other. A room with a skirting/baseboard does not have to have a cornice. If there is a cornice, however, there should always be a skirting/baseboard as well to balance the room. A deep, encrusted cornice would look top heavy in a low-ceilinged room. Such rooms should have small, slender cornices and skirting/baseboards to match. A room with a sense of grandeur needs a strong, rich cornice and an equally impressive skirting/baseboard.

Adding cornices, skirting/baseboards, picture rails, and dado rails gently furnishes the shell of your room. They soften the hard edges – a cornice, for example, removes the harsh right angle where the wall meets the ceiling. Picture rails look cosy and make it easy to hang pictures without drilling holes and ruining your walls. Dado rails give an opportunity for changing the colour or style of decorating above or below the division. They can be made of wood, painted simply, or given a sumptuous faux finish, such as tortoiseshell or malachite.

Such additions do not suit all rooms. In a minimalist room, anything more than a slim cornice and a plain skirting/baseboard would clutter a space intended to be perfectly simple and pure.

Wall dividers

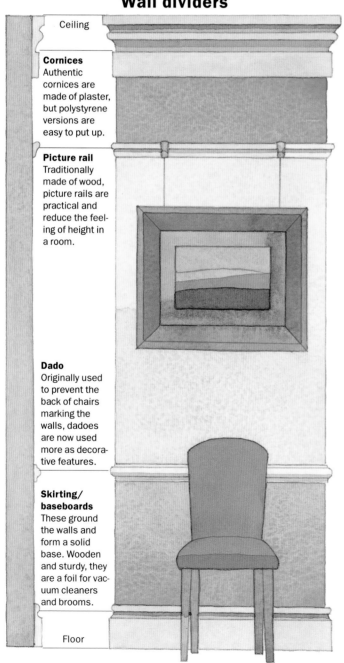

Ceiling

Cornices
Authentic cornices are made of plaster, but polystyrene versions are easy to put up.

Picture rail
Traditionally made of wood, picture rails are practical and reduce the feeling of height in a room.

Dado
Originally used to prevent the back of chairs marking the walls, dadoes are now used more as decorative features.

Skirting/ baseboards
These ground the walls and form a solid base. Wooden and sturdy, they are a foil for vacuum cleaners and brooms.

Floor

DADOES

Ideas for enhancing wooden dadoes or creating dado borders

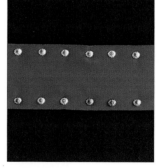

Ribbon dado
A false dado, made of ribbon and brass studs, has been added to this fabric wall.

Enhanced woodwork
A wooden dado has been enhanced by picking out the moulding in gold metallic paint.

False dado
A band of painted tortoise-shell, with narrow gold borders, has been added in the dado position.

Paint effect
Here the wooden dado has been dragged with acrylic yellow glaze over white vinyl silk/satin latex.

Average room

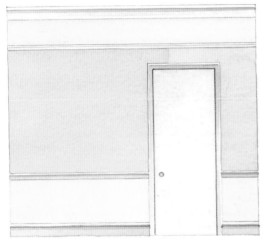

In an average 2.7m (9ft) room, the skirting/baseboard and cornice should not be more than about 15cm (6in) deep and the dado 75–90cm (30–36in) from the floor. Horizontal divisions may reduce the feeling of space but add character and give scope for different paint treatments.

Tall room

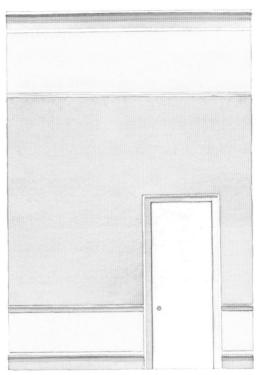

In a taller room of 4.2m (14 ft) or more, the cornice and skirting/baseboard can be deeper and more substantial. The two should be kept in proportion. The dado rail remains the same height from the floor as in the average room, but the picture rail can be placed higher as desired.

Dynamic dividers

Deliberately bold and eye-catching, dadoes and picture rails have been given special treatment in this home. Painted in strong colours, they attract attention and accentuate the proportions of the walls. A diamond, trellis-like pattern is repeated in different colourways, linking the rooms.

Doors, windows, and fireplaces

IN MOST ROOMS at least two walls are broken up by doors, windows, and perhaps a fireplace, which give visual relief as well as serving their practical purposes. Decoration can highlight these features or help them blend into the walls.

Doors

Every room has to have a door, unless it is simply entered through an archway or opening from another room. The size of the door should be appropriate for the proportions of the room. Grand rooms in large houses may have large double doors with as many as four gilded panels on each. Architraves on such doors may be up to 36cm (14in) wide, with several lines of intricate moulding.

Most of us live in normal houses with average 2m (6ft 6in) doors. These can be simply painted, treated with an effect such as distressing, or woodgrained or stencilled to compliment the walls. Consider whether you want the door to blend with the walls or make an impact. A plain flush door, for example, can be made more interesting with trompe l'oeil panels to add a sense of age to a room.

Windows

Dens in windowless cellars and basements can look cosy, but may feel claustrophobic. My favourite rooms have plenty of windows and natural light and I like to throw the windows open to let in air and rejuvenate the room. I believe that the more windows, and light, a house has, the merrier and more optimistic the atmosphere.

Window frames don't need special effects. Most will be covered by curtains or blinds for much of the time and look best just painted or vanished. You don't always have to paint window frames white or cream – try matching them to the walls or painting them a contrasting colour.

Fireplaces

Few things beat the look and smell of a roaring fire on a cold night. Fireplaces are now a luxury for most of us but they still make a fine focal point for a room. Unless you are lucky enough to have a real marble surround, make your fireplace more interesting by painting it or applying a faux finish such as marbling, stone, malachite, or frottage.

Marble fantasy
Unashamedly vivid and gorgeous, this red fireplace would warm the room, even without a fire being lit. The painted marble is pure fantasy – it imitates the texture of the real thing but goes for wild colour, which stands out boldly against the deep blue walls.

Blending into the background

In this unusual example of stencilling, the design has been continued onto the doors and even architraves as well as all over the walls, giving the room a magical, fairytale quality. The explosion of pattern has the effect of camouflaging the doors so that they blend into the walls.

A framed window

A curtain over this little recessed window would look fussy and be in the way. Instead, the owner has chosen to leave the window bare and create a paint-effect border to frame the alcove and set it off from the surrounding red walls. The paint has been gently distressed to make it resemble naturally aged wood.

DOORS

Decorative ideas for door treatments

The borders of the panels on this door have been picked out in a rich blue.

Trompe l'oeil panels have been applied to liven up a plain, flush door.

A handle and moulding picked out in terracotta adds interest to a white door.

This door has been painted in strong blue to set off the deep orange colourwash next to it.

This basic wooden door has been woodgrained to make it look like rich mahogany.

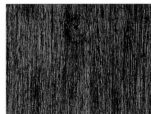

Distressing is an excellent effect to use on doors and other woodwork.

FIREPLACES

Ideas for decorating a simple wooden fireplace

Many fireplaces are made of marble so a painted marble finish will have an authentic look for a fraction of the price.

A sumptuous, elaborate faux finish such as malachite looks wonderfully punchy and theatrical used on a fireplace.

Colour

LUXURIOUS AND SENSUOUS, colour is a wonderful thing. It excites the eye, exudes energy and carries hidden messages. Unlike most luxuries, colour is affordable, available to us all for the price of a pot of paint. Something to revel in, colour creates atmosphere and demands reactions. That said, the power of the pure white room should not be underestimated. White can inspire and elevate the senses as much as stronger colours and it lends an inimitable simplicity to a room.

Inspiration

Mary Gilliatt, a friend and author of numerous decorating books, described the colour she wanted me to paint her sitting room as 'a nebulous combination of amber and cinnamon'. She was describing a sensation rather than an established colour and it is often these ambiguous, hard-to-define colours that hold most interest and pleasure. Inspiration for colours can come from anywhere – from the spine of a book, the petal of a flower, the face of a mountain. Precious stones and culinary spices are rewarding sources. The results of such ideas can be both subtle and spirited, interesting and yet easy to live with.

Blue harmony

Walls colourwashed with faded blue, and subtle shades of blue on the floor and door give this hallway an atmosphere of quiet harmony. The colours blend together seamlessly – the only bright blue is on the decorative skirting/baseboard.

Warm and cool colours

Warm colours are immediate and strong and appear to advance toward you from the wall. Cool colours recede and have less impact on the room.

Deep red, a striking pure orange, and a saffron-inspired yellow – these are all warm colours that embrace the senses and create a joyous atmosphere in a room.

A serene pale blue, a mellow green, and a deep cream, these are all relaxing cool colours, which soothe the nerves. They are timeless and undemanding.

Subtle and bright colours

Subtle colours are inspired by natural, organic substances and are generally softened with white. Bright colours are bold and brave. Never subtle, they are full of life and optimism.

Rich green, solid burgundy, and handsome blue with a tinge of grey are all subtle, earthy colours that would look good in period or modern homes.

A bright emerald green, brilliant yellow, and vital blue, these primary colours are all brimming with energy and fun.

Juxtaposing colours

USING TWO OR MORE COLOURS together in a room can be tremendously successful, whether the result is a harmony of creams, beiges, and browns or a cacophony of strident, contrasting shades. Look at the colours carefully and think about how they affect each other and whether they work together. Similar colours should have some sort of relationship of colour or tone. Contrasting colours should not cancel each other out in their vibrancy.

Pairs of similar colours

Related, similar colours work well together and create a subtle, harmonious effect in a room.

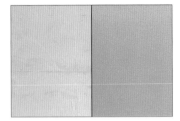

These two shades of yellow – a dark and a frottaged paler hue – flatter one another.

These two greens contrast in strength but have a natural union because of their shared pigment.

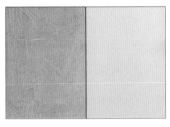

Lilac and pale blue compliment each other beautifully and do not compete.

Pairs of contrasting colours

Contrasting colours have a powerful, dramatic effect. Such vivid and surprising combinations stimulate the senses.

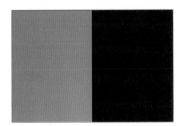

Red and black are always explosive, thrilling partners.

The strength of this yellow and the depth of the blue make an effective combination.

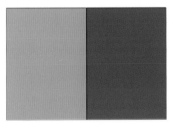

This orange and blue green are a softer, gentler example of contrasting colour but still vibrant.

The power of colour

Rich, orange-red walls transform this hallway, which leads into a sunny yellow dining room – both rooms are a testament to the power of colour. The walls are painted in emulsion/ latex, with no special effects. The finished look is lively and eye-catching simply because of the confident use of strong colour.

Texture

TEXTURED WALLS give a room extra substance and interest. Rough plaster, perfect for camouflaging uneven walls, is the most common textured finish. The effect is unsophisticated, yet attractive and welcoming. Ideal in a rustic setting, rough plaster could also form a pleasing contrast with sleek, modern kitchen fittings. Other examples of textured wallcoverings include tiling and the use of tongue and groove – wooden strips that are closely butted up to one another and attached to the wall. Some kinds of wallpaper are textured, and fabric lends walls a sensuous, cushioned feel.

Painted texture

Alternatively you can create the look of texture in paint, with simple techniques such as frottage, ragging, and marbling. These are not three-dimensional effects, but they have a textured organic appearance, which engages the eye and gives a room an air of importance.

Rough plaster

A lick of paint over a rough plaster finish lends a medieval air to this wall and makes a perfect foil for the neat alcove. The textured effect is timeless and charming, perfectly enhanced by candlelight.

Three-dimensional texture

Tongue and groove, tiles, and rough plaster all give a three-dimensional quality to a room and add character and interest. All three are surprisingly inexpensive to install.

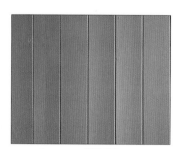

The addition of woodwork, such as tongue and groove, gives a feeling of warmth and age, particularly if the wood is distressed.

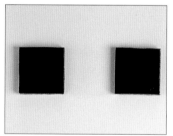

These bold blue tiles on stark white walls are used here purely to provide textural interest and linear beauty.

A pale terracotta colourwash is the perfect finish for this rough plaster wall.

Visual texture

Frottage, ragged stripes, and marbling are three ways of adding visual texture to your walls. They all provide depth and contrast and so give the impression of texture.

This lilac frottage is soft and light and can baffle the eye. The clues of how the look is achieved are hard to find.

Ragging provides a softly textured look, which is highlighted by the pattern of these subtly coloured wide stripes.

Marbled blocks provide a cool and refreshing texture, redolent of the real thing. Mistakes can easily be turned into interesting streaks.

Pattern

From cave paintings to graffiti, pattern has always been part of human creativity. There is something immensely satisfying about a symmetrical, balanced design. Stencilling is the easiest way to bring wholly original pattern to your home. Any shape in the world may be drawn, traced onto stencil card, and put on your wall in the pattern you want. Alternatively, there is now an immense range of wallpapers in every imaginable design.

Traditionally, large patterns are thought to be too overwhelming for small spaces and are kept for big rooms. I like to encourage people to try ample, dramatic patterns in smaller rooms, where they can look spectacular.

Mixing patterns

Patterns can be used together successfully. Here, a geometric trompe l'oeil hanging sits well with the floral designs nearby because of the simplicity of the patterns and their harmonious, earthy colours.

Subtle pattern

Understated pattern can be most rewarding. Large areas of wall may be covered with something soft and unobtrusive without it seeming overwhelming.

Colourwashing creates a soft, basket-weave pattern that is random yet pleasing to the eye.

This traditional stencil design needs to be positioned with precision to look its best. Stencil and background are close in colour.

This wallpaper is strong in colour but softly patterned. The geometric motif forms a closely knit, straightforward design.

Dramatic pattern

Dramatic pattern with a sense of theatre can be amusing and light-hearted – a must for some parts of the house.

This urn-patterned wallpaper is both detailed and robust. The colours are clearly monochrome but the effect is not dull.

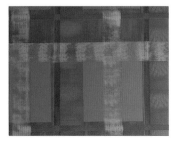

Created with only three colours, this painted tartan makes a dramatic impact. Inspired by a real tartan, it is not a slavish copy.

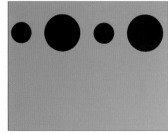

Bold contrasting colours make this simple pattern interesting. Don't over do it – one row of stencil circles is sufficient here.

Style Directory

The Hall

HALLS GIVE THE FIRST IMPRESSION of a home. Cottage or castle, apartment or penthouse, the hall is a place of greetings and farewells. On entry, the hall sets the mood; on departure, it holds the memory. Although sometimes treated as an afterthought, the hall links the other rooms of the house and deserves equal attention in its decoration. It is an ideal place to try more complex effects, such as trompe l'oeil or marbled blocks, where there is little furniture to get in the way.

A hall does not have to be lofty and grand to look welcoming and glamorous. Richly painted walls or bold wallpaper immediately appear warm and friendly. A deep coral, for example, makes an ideal backdrop for carefully hung clusters of pictures, a slim coatstand, and a mirror. Mirrors are always effective in a hall. In a cramped passage, a mirror increases space and light as well as giving guests the chance to check their appearance.

Large, lofty halls with generous staircases look best with an airy, timeless decoration. Pale terracotta and yellows are favourites. Such halls also lend themselves to furnishing with bookshelves, wooden benches, stands of flowers, and larger, weightier mirrors.

Elegant stone blocks

Airy and elegant, this hallway has a strong architectural feel that is softened by the warm sandstone colours used on the painted blocks above the dado. These blocks, accentuated with dark and light shading lines, add a gracious formality to the hall. Their geometric shapes are offset by the archway and the semicircular window above the door.

Marbled grandeur, above

This grand entrance to the Parisian house that once belonged to
the Duke and Duchess of Windsor is theatrical in style. The marbled areas are executed in a painterly fashion and the glowing
colours make this a welcoming area, despite its classic elegance.
Few homes aspire to such grandeur, but the colours and shapes
used here could be echoed in simpler surroundings.

Stencilled tongue and groove, right

Simplicity at its best, this stencilled, tongue and grooved hallway
makes a charming entrance to the house. The stylized, primitive
design is used only on the top part of the wall and the lower half is
painted in the same blue-grey as used for the stencils. The two are
divided by a deep purple dado band which steadies the stencilling.

KEY TO THE TECHNIQUES

Marbled blocks

The wall was prepared in white **vinyl silk/satin latex** (see p. 72). Block shapes were measured and drawn onto the wall (see p. 78) and **marbling** (see pp. 98–99) was applied with two acrylic glazes – grey and pale ochre.

The skirting/baseboard was painted in white **quick-drying/ acrylic latex eggshell** (see p. 72). A grey and umber glaze was **distressed** (see p. 108).

Key stencil

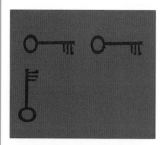

The wall above the dado was painted with red **matt emulsion/latex** (see p. 72) and **stencilled** (see pp. 94–97) with a simple key design in deep blue-green matt emulsion/ latex.

The wall under the dado was painted with blue-green **matt emulsion/latex** (see p. 72) and the woodwork in a deeper mix of the colour in **oil eggshell** (see p. 72).

Wide stripes and woodgrained door

The wall was painted in white **vinyl silk/satin latex** (see p. 72, then **ragged** (see p. 86) with a green acrylic glaze. **Wide stripes** (see pp. 88–89) were applied in the same green glaze and ragged.

The door and skirting/base-board were painted in cinnamon **quick-drying/acrylic latex eggshell** (see p. 72). Both were **woodgrained** (see pp. 100–101) with brown acrylic glaze. A coat of **varnish** (see p. 73) was applied.

Marbled blocks

The effect of this marbled wall is airy and lofty, with a cool, soft look created by the different depths of colour in the blocks. This treatment is particularly suited to hallways and staircases, but it also suits bathrooms and dining rooms. The colours used here are undemanding and easy to live with. An advantage of marbled effects is that you can add a hint of colour, such as green, blue, or umber, while still retaining a neutral look.

Key stencil

This light-hearted example shows just how versatile stencilling can be. You can produce any shape and repeat it to make a unique design. The simple key motifs used here echo the use of this area for hanging the household's keys. Strong colours and an element of fun make this idea most suitable for a smaller rather than larger area, such as a lobby or entrance hall before the main body of the house.

Wide stripes and woodgrained door

These stripes in two shades of green create a quiet, subtle look. The darker green stripe is simply two layers of the green applied over the whole wall. This is a smart, sophisticated effect that is ideal for a hallway, but it would also suit an elegant dining room, or a masculine bedroom, or study. The warm brown tones of the woodgrained door and skirting/baseboard provide the perfect compliment to the two shades of green.

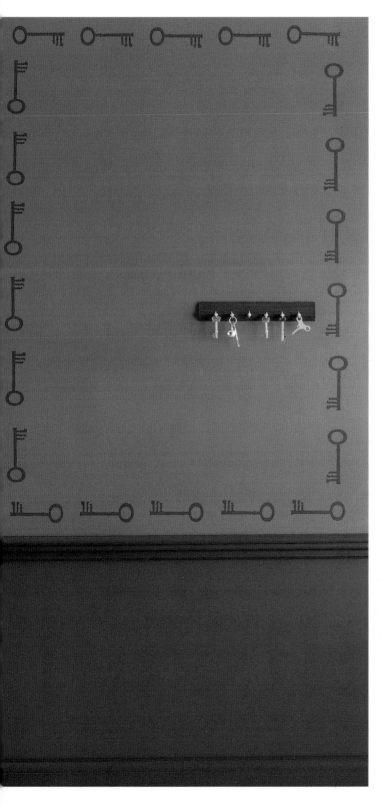

KEY TO THE TECHNIQUES

Trompe l'oeil umbrella stand

The wall was painted in blue **matt emulsion/latex** (see p. 72).

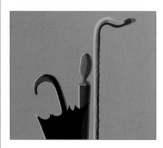

The door and skirting/base-board were painted in rich cream **oil eggshell** (see p. 72). The mouldings on the door panels were **picked out** (see p. 73) in the same blue as the walls.

The **trompe l'oeil** (see pp. 104–105) umbrella stand was drawn on paper and traced onto the wall and skirting/baseboard. It was painted, then highlighted with greys and creams to create the three-dimensional effect.

Pale wide stripes

The wall was painted with white **vinyl silk/satin latex** (see p. 72) and **ragged** (see p. 86) with cream acrylic glaze. The wall below the dado was given a second coat of ragged glaze.

Wide paint-effect stripes (see p. 89) were added above the dado. Woodwork was painted in cream quick-drying/acrylic latex eggshell and **dragged** (see p. 84) with beige glaze.

Découpage maps

The maps were pasted to the wall as **découpage** (see pp. 122–123). The butterflies were added at the end and the whole wall was given several coats of protective acrylic **varnish** (see p. 73).

The skirting/baseboard was painted with white **oil eggshell** (see p. 72), and a découpage butterfly added.

Trompe l'oeil umbrella stand

Trompe l'oeil brings a ray of light relief and frivolity to this factual world. You might expect to find an umbrella stand beside a hall door, so the image is undemanding, yet entertaining. Less is more is a key principle to remember when considering trompe l'oeil effects – don't overdo it. You don't have to be an artist to attempt trompe l'oeil – images can be copied – but they do have to be carefully painted if they are to look effective.

Pale wide stripes

Soft stripes in shades of cream create a tranquil atmosphere to welcome you into the house. Ragging adds textural interest to the subtle colours and the plain area below the dado rail steadies the effect. This is an elegant, classic look, which would be be both practical and easy to live with. Maintain the smart look by using similar neutral colours for curtains and sofas. Alternatively, brighten it up and make it less formal with furnishings in primary colours.

Découpage maps

This is a refreshingly lively example of découpage, ideal for armchair travellers. The effect created is that of a highly original wallpaper. The maps have been thoughtfully arranged with an eye to both colour and shape, and the butterflies provide an attractive linking device that keeps the overall look from being too boxy. This effect is best suited to a hall where there is the minimum of furniture to confuse the eye.

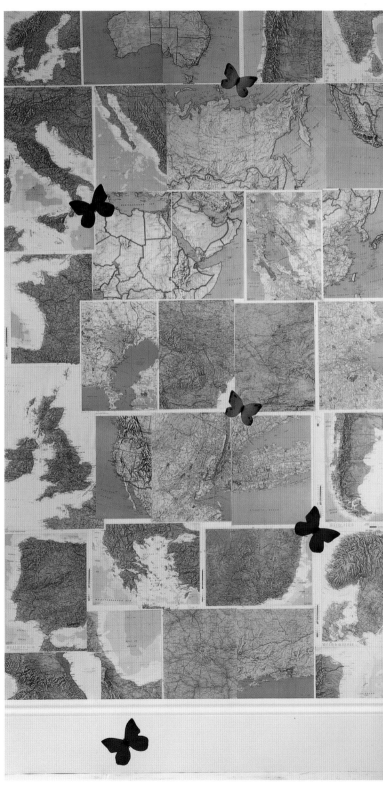

KEY TO THE TECHNIQUES

Black stencil on red

The wall was painted with red **matt emulsion/latex** (see p. 72). The rows of **stencilling** (see pp. 94–97) at cornice and dado level were applied with black matt emulsion/latex.

The skirting/baseboard was painted in black **oil eggshell** (see p. 72) to match the stencilling.

Bull stencil on green

The wall was painted in soft green **matt emulsion/latex** (see p. 72) and **stencilled** (see pp. 94–97) in a darker shade of green.

The skirting/baseboard was painted in the same green used for the stencilling but in **oil eggshell** (see p. 72).

Black and white urn wallpaper

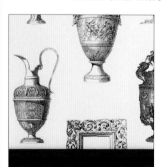

The wall was prepared and **wallpapered** (see pp. 114–119). The skirting/baseboard was painted in black **oil eggshell** (see p. 72).

Black stencil on red

The contrasting colours on this wall give a strong, straightforward look. The two rows of stencilling create the illusion of a cornice and dado on the wall, breaking up the expanse of red most effectively. The cornice stencil has a fine Gothic design, which gains strength from the solidity of black on red, while the lower band is simple and strong. This bold effect is most suited to a hall but would also look good in a dining room.

Bull stencil on green

A light-hearted design, these bull stencils could create a refreshing reminder of green fields and clean country air in the small hallway of a city house or would work equally well on the walls of a farmhouse. The stencils should be applied in a casual yet balanced arrangement and the design should not look too regimented. Note the slight variations in numbers and levels, and the bull facing in the opposite direction to the rest of the herd.

Black and white urn wallpaper

This wallpaper is a clever combination of classic and modern. The designs of the urns and picture frames have a classic elegance, while the stark black and white lends a modern touch. This bold pattern has an architectural feel that is best suited to hall areas, where there is little furniture to conflict with the design. It looks wonderful in large airy halls and is also effective in smaller lobby areas.

The Kitchen

BEFORE DESIGNING your kitchen, think about how much time you are likely to spend in it. This will help you judge whether you want a look that is functional or comfortable, practical, or even outlandish.

Having painted many kitchens, I feel that they fall into two broad categories. The first includes family kitchens, rooms that are the centre of the household, where people relax as well as cook. These kitchens are large and cosy, with a lived-in atmosphere. They may house a sofa, a television, and almost certainly a big table. Walls must be durable and easy to repair, so emulsion/latex, colourwashes, tiles, and light, bright effects are all appropriate.

The second main type belongs to the professional single person or couple. This kitchen may be small and functional. It may contain labour-saving devices, such as a microwave, but rarely a dog basket. High stools replace squashy sofas. The walls of such a kitchen receive less of a battering than those of the family-style room and so a more exotic treatment can be risked. Chinese red lacquered walls, for example, tortoiseshelled stripes on black, or even simple emulsion/latex in a rich, dark colour.

A practical finish

The neatly tiled walls in this kitchen are both attractive and easy to clean. White tiles make a plain background for the work area and the *batterie de cuisine*, while the black and white tiles add an Arabic flavour and create a lively look on the room divider wall.

Bold stripes

The wide painted stripes dominate this kitchen-dining area, and create
a fresh, light-hearted atmosphere. Stripes are generally thought to
accentuate height and in this, already high-ceilinged, room the effect
is still successful. The subtle distressed finish of the dresser and table
is deliberately low-key so that these furnishings do not compete with the
bold paintwork. Bright blue and yellow china adds sunny warmth and
informality to the scene.

KEY TO THE TECHNIQUES

Colourwashed rough plaster

The wall was covered with a **rough plaster** finish (see p. 109) and painted with a coat of watered-down white **matt emulsion/latex** and one of white **vinyl silk/satin latex** (see p. 72). It was **colourwashed** (see pp. 82–83) in an acrylic glaze mixed with burnt sienna, ochre, and raw umber pigments.

The door and skirting/baseboard were painted in off-white **oil eggshell** (see p. 72).

Blue tiles on white emulsion

The wall was painted in white **matt emulsion/latex** (see p. 72). Two rows of **tiles** (see pp. 110–113) were then stuck to the wall. The skirting/baseboard was painted in white **oil eggshell** (see p. 72).

Primitive animal wallpaper

The wall was prepared and **wallpapered** (see pp. 114–119) and given a coat of flat acrylic **varnish** (see p. 73).

The skirting/baseboard was painted in cream **oil eggshell** (see p. 72) to match the colour of the animal motifs on the wallpaper.

Colourwashed rough plaster

The textured rough plaster finish, covered with a soft terracotta colourwash, adds warmth and character to the room. The look achieved is informal and unsophisticated, ideal for country kitchens and dining rooms. Because the effect is deliberately uneven, dirty marks do not show up easily — always useful in a kitchen. The smooth creamy finish on the door and the skirting/baseboard acts as a perfect foil for the rough warmth of the walls.

Blue tiles on white emulsion

Refreshingly simple, plain white walls look both classic and modern and create a clean, uncluttered atmosphere for a kitchen. Here, the lines of dark blue tiles provide a dramatic focus and give a sense of order and design to the room. These tiles are purely decorative and do not fulfil their usual role of protecting the wall from splashes or grease. Although white emulsion/latex walls are easily marked, they are equally easy to re-touch.

Primitive animal wallpaper

Wallpaper is a decorative finish for any room. In a kitchen a coat of flat acrylic varnish over the paper allows the surface to be wiped clean – useful in households with young children. The animals on this paper are inspired by African and Ancient Egyptian paintings, giving a charmingly naive look. It is a repeat pattern, but the differences in size between the tall giraffe and the low-lying crocodile keep it from looking too regular.

KEY TO THE TECHNIQUES

Yellow and white wide stripes

The wall was first painted with white **matt emulsion/latex** (see p. 72). The **stripes** (see pp. 88–89) were painted with two coats of yellow matt emulsion/latex. Walls and units were varnished with flat acrylic **varnish** (see p. 73).

Fruit découpage on green

The wall was painted in soft green **matt emulsion/latex** (see p. 72). The fruits were cut out from wrapping paper and applied as **découpage** (see pp. 122–123). Several coats of acrylic **varnish** (see p. 73) were applied to the découpage.

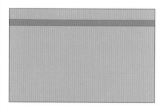

The orange border **stripes** were marked with masking tape (see p. 78). Stripes were painted with orange vinyl silk/satin latex, using a stippling brush.

The skirting/baseboard was painted in orange **oil eggshell** (see p. 72) to match the border stripes.

Pale blue walls with blue tiles

The wall was painted in pale blue **matt emulsion/latex** (see p. 72). The skirting/baseboard was painted in white **oil eggshell** (see p. 72).

The arrangement of the **tiles** (see pp. 110–113) was carefully worked out. The tiles were then stuck around the alcove.

Yellow and white wide stripes

Painting a room with strong-coloured stripes on a white ground is not for the faint-hearted. The effect is bold and strident and gives the room great vigour and energy. A kitchen painted in this style would always have a cheery golden glow. Large kitchen units can often look block-like and unattractive, but keeping the same colour scheme as the walls makes the units less obtrusive and unites them with the rest of the room.

Fruit découpage on green

The strong colour and photographic clarity of the images used make this an unusually fresh and stimulating example of découpage. The green base makes a suitably muted background and the horizontal orange stripes hold the border and give it a definite edge, while providing a contrast with the green. Ration the images you use for a clean and bright effect that is in stark contrast to the sometimes gloomy look of old-fashioned découpage.

Pale blue walls with blue tiles

A gentle blue matt emulsion/latex with a hint of lavender gives this kitchen a calm, tranquil atmosphere that would be easy to live in. Patterned tiles in stronger tones of blue are used to make a decorative border for the recessed shelves. The tiles create a focal point in the room and transform the simple shelves, creating an ideal spot for the display of beautiful objects.

KEY TO THE TECHNIQUES

Yellow, red, and green kitchen

The wall and door knobs were painted in yellow **matt emulsion/latex** (see p. 72).

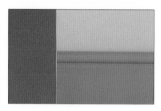

The dado, skirting/baseboard, and unit doors and tops were painted in **oil eggshell** (see p. 72). The unit tops and door-knobs were **varnished** (see p. 73).

Stone blocks and distressed wood

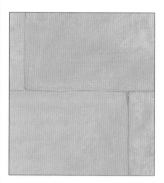

The wall above the dado was painted with white **vinyl silk/satin latex** (see p. 72). The **blocks** (see p. 78) were measured and drawn out. Each block was painted with grey, umber, and ochre acrylic glaze and **frottaged** (see pp. 106–107).

The dado and panelling were painted with **blue vinyl silk/satin latex** (see p. 72). A dark blue acrylic glaze was then applied and **dragged** (see p. 84). The wood was then **distressed** (see p. 108).

Melon and cherry stencil

The wall was painted with yellow **matt emulsion/latex** (see p. 72). The melons and cherries were **stencilled** (see pp. 94–97) in red and green.

The door and skirting/baseboard were painted in grey-green **oil eggshell** (see p. 72).

Yellow, red, and green kitchen

Sunny yellow walls and brilliantly coloured units bring immense vitality to this kitchen. The bold colour scheme would help to brighten a room that has little natural light and is particularly suitable for a family kitchen-dining area with a relaxed, friendly feel. Despite their frivolous air, the colourful varnished surfaces in this kitchen are practical and easy to wipe clean.

Stone blocks and distressed wood

This is a rustic look, suited to a rambling country kitchen with a big wooden table and comfortable chairs. Although the upper part of the wall is painted and frottaged to look like cool stone blocks, the colours give it a warm feeling. The rich blue panelling below steadies the effect and adds interest and texture. Easy to live with, this look copes well with the odd bump and scratch.

Melon and cherry stencil

Fresh and uncomplicated, this stencil treatment is a quick and relatively easy way to bring a touch of individuality to a plain kitchen. Bright, bold stencils like these fruit designs could be overwhelming if used all over a room, but they make a wonderful border around the door and skirting/baseboard. Less is more can be a good rule to remember when using stencils. The pale yellow background is subtle yet warm and allows the stencils to dominate.

The Dining Room

Nowadays, many homes do not have the luxury of a separate dining room. Sitting and dining room may have have been knocked into one or the eating area could be part of the kitchen. In homes that do have a dining room, it may be used only in the evening, so provides a wonderful opportunity for being adventurous with the decoration. In a room that you don't use all day and every day you can afford to create a bolder and more sumptuous look than elsewhere in the house. A look that is tailormade for flickering candlelight and conversations that last into the night. Try dramatic stencilled designs, painted stripes or tartan, and bold colours.

Strident, brightly coloured decoration encourages an informal atmosphere, a room where friends are entertained and people feel relaxed. Rich, deep hues, perhaps with paint effects such as ragging, are cosy and inviting and particularly suited to rooms used mainly in the evening.

For more formal dining rooms you might prefer to decorate in lighter, more neutral tones, which compliment elegant furniture. In any style of dining room, take care with lighting. It should focus on the table and allow diners to see what they are eating but not be too bright.

Dining rooms which are used all day and every day, or eating areas that are part of the kitchen or sitting room need a slightly different treatment. A less demanding look, such as a warm colourwash that glows by day and holds impact at night, would be one solution. A room where young children are to eat and perhaps play in during the day needs something that is easy to wipe clean – perhaps a subtly patterned wallpaper that has been given a coat of protective varnish, or simple matt emulsion/latex that is easy to re-touch when necessary.

Simple colour, left

Slabs of colour – pale green, purple, and yellow – have been used here to create a simple but lively look, a perfect example of what can be achieved with matt emulsion/latex. No effects are needed. The interest comes from the combination of colours.

Classic elegance, above

This is an evening room with an elegant feel. Above the dado is a classic wallpaper in rich glowing colours. Below are painted panels with trompe l'oeil frames which give an opulent look to the room. Alternate panels have been painted with symmetrical stylized designs.

KEY TO THE TECHNIQUES

Geometric stencil and malachite

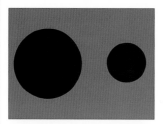

The wall was painted in green **matt emulsion/latex** (see p. 72) and **stencil** (see pp. 94–97) circles added in black matt emulsion/latex. The skirting/baseboard was painted in black **oil eggshell** (see p. 72).

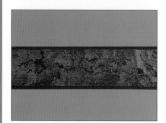

The position of the malachite dado band was **measured and marked** (see p. 78). The **malachite effect** (see p. 103) was created with dark blue acrylic glaze and given a coat of acrylic **varnish** (see p. 73).

Metallic stencils on ragged wall

The wall was painted in blue **vinyl silk/satin latex** (see p. 72) and **ragged** (see p. 86) in dark blue acrylic glaze. Circles and diamonds were **stencilled** (see pp. 94–97) with silver paint. The skirting/baseboard was prepared with **quick-drying/ acrylic latex eggshell** (see p. 72) and **dragged** (see p. 84) with blue acrylic glaze.

Strong colourwash

The wall was painted in white **vinyl silk/satin latex** (see p. 72). It was then **colourwashed** (see pp. 82–83) with an orange acrylic glaze and brushed out with a dry 15cm (6in) brush.

The door and skirting/baseboard were painted in dark blue **oil eggshell** (see p. 72).

Geometric stencil and malachite

The combination of positive colours and strong shapes makes this a striking, unconventional look for a dining room. The bright green is fresh and stimulating, and the dark stencils and decorative malachite break up the expanse and add perspective. This style would be an ideal treatment for a dark gloomy room. Indeed it is perfect for rooms with little natural light – sun streaming through the windows would lessen the impact of the strong colours.

Metallic stencils on ragged wall

This is a dramatic colour scheme, which would lend a sense of occasion to any interior. It is best suited to a room that is used mostly at night. The combination of deep blue and metallic silver create an elegant, sophisticated atmosphere, perfectly enhanced by flickering candlelight. Metallic stencilling demands precision. Measure and apply it with great care for a striking, bold finish.

Strong colourwash

Colourwashing with deep, rich colours makes a perfect finish for living or dining rooms. It looks smart by day and warm by night. The stronger the pigment added to the glaze, the more powerful the brush strokes appear. Here, the use of a strong orange on white creates a vibrant, luminous look. The dark blue woodwork provides contrast and definition. This colour scheme would make a perfect background for large, framed posters of modern art.

KEY TO THE TECHNIQUES

Tartan

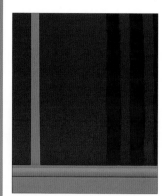

The wall was painted in green **matt emulsion/latex** (see p. 72). Foam rollers and burgundy emulsion/latex were used to create the **tartan** pattern (see pp. 92–93). The narrow creamy yellow lines were stippled. The skirting/baseboard was painted in creamy yellow **oil eggshell** (see p. 72).

Red ragged wall with gold

The wall was painted in white **vinyl silk/satin latex** (see p. 72). A deep red acrylic glaze was applied and **ragged**, then **softened** (see p. 86) with a badger brush. Several layers of glaze were applied to achieve a sumptuous depth.

The woodwork was painted in deep red **oil eggshell** (see p. 72). Once dry, part of the moulding on both was **picked out** in gold (see p. 73).

Blue stipple

The wall was painted in white **vinyl silk/satin latex** (see p. 72). A blue acrylic glaze was added and **stippled** (see p. 85). The stipple was then **flicked** with white (see p. 100).

The skirting/baseboard was painted in white **oil eggshell** (see p. 72) and stippled in blue and flicked with white as above. More flicking was done here to give a greater density of white than on the wall.

Tartan

Flamboyant and colourful, tartan makes a dramatic wall treatment for a dining room. Try to maintain an echo of the colour and style of traditional plaid, but your painted version does not have to be an exact representation. The soft burgundy checks in this example re-create the texture of wool, while the crisply executed golden lines in the pattern link with the skirting/baseboard to add balance.

Red ragged wall with gold

Nothing could look warmer and more welcoming than these rich red walls. The moody ragging softens the bold colour and lends texture and depth. The gold highlights on the moulding of the dado and skirting/baseboard provide an important contrast to the red and add a touch of opulence to the room. This is a cosy and inviting dining room that would encourage festive gatherings lasting late into the night.

Blue stipple

Stippling can look flat and neat, but this blue and white example has a rougher, more open feel, resembling a starry sky. The millions of tiny dots made by the stippling brush look lively and almost three-dimensional, while the white flicked over the stipple adds freshness and exuberance. The effect is completed by a skirting/baseboard stippled in the same rich blue glaze as the walls, but flicked with more white to provide a slight contrast.

KEY TO THE TECHNIQUES

Green baize wall with ribbon dado

To make the **fabric panel** (see pp. 120–121), a wooden frame was attached to the wall. Wadding and fabric were stapled to the frame.

A strip of wide red ribbon was glued to the baize in the **dado position** (see p. 78). Two rows of brass studs were hammered onto the ribbon.

Tree wallpaper

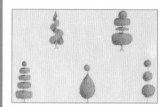

The wall above the dado was **wallpapered** (see pp. 114–119) in the usual way.

The wall below the dado was painted in pale yellow **matt emulsion/latex** (see p. 72).

The dado and skirting/baseboard were painted in black **oil eggshell** (see p. 72).

Black and gold stencilled squares

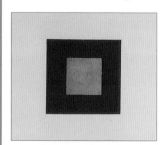

The wall was first painted in pink **matt emulsion/latex** (see p. 72). The outer and inner squares were **stencilled** (see pp. 94–97) with black and gold **metallic paint** (see p. 71) .

The skirting/baseboard was painted in black **oil eggshell** (see p. 72) and the moulding **picked out** (see p. 73) in gold **metallic paint**.

Green baize wall with ribbon dado

Covering walls in fabric, such as baize or felt, softens the atmosphere of a room. The fabric absorbs sound and gives a physically warm feel. Here, the effect of the dark green baize with the red ribbon detail and rows of brass studs is extremely luxurious. This look is ideal for a dining room that is used mostly in the evenings, a place to linger in by candlelight, sipping brandy and black coffee.

Tree wallpaper

Although the trees featured are clearly masterpieces of the art of topiary, this wallpaper has a simple graphic look with its varied shapes. Painting the wall below the dado pale yellow steadies the room and keeps the effect from looking too busy. The striking black skirting/baseboard and dado add a note of bold sophistication well suited to a daytime dining room.

Black and gold stencilled squares

Wonderfully unconventional, this dining room has a 1930s feel. The colour combination is punchy and vital – not a look to be ignored. The stencilled gold inner squares have a reflecting, metallic effect and make an exciting contrast to the matt black outer squares on which they sit. The bright pink wall behind them is warm and vibrant, an ideal setting for bold furnishings and animated conversation round the dinner table.

The Sitting Room

IN MANY HOMES it is the sitting room that is most on show. It is the room used for entertaining friends and it usually houses favourite pictures and items of furniture. In some households, life centres on the kitchen and perhaps on a family room or den. The sitting room can then be separate and more formal – an area where children and clutter are not allowed. If such a room is rarely used it can feel chilly and unwelcoming. Counteract this by treating the walls with warm, inviting colours and using richly coloured textiles to create a cosy atmosphere.

Most of us do not have the luxury of extra space and the sitting room is where everything happens. Here you do not need to think about enticing people in but making sure that the room is one that you feel comfortable in.

For me, this means fresh flowers, strong colours, and the minimum of clutter. Others feel happier with a wealth of ornaments and cushions. A sitting room should be a place to relax and feel at home, so if this means painting the walls bright pink and providing hammocks instead of sofas, have the confidence to follow your desires.

Peaceful white

Sometimes plain white walls are all that are needed. The rugs and furnishings of this sitting room are perfectly complimented by simple white emulsion/latex and a stone floor, giving the room a peaceful, quiet look. There is a strong sense of light and the outdoors, despite the fact that no windows are visible.

Palm tree stencils

A bold all-over stencil design is made subtle by the use of similar sandy colours. The effect is almost one of dancing shadows on the wall. The warm, luxurious look is completed by the Middle Eastern feel of the furnishings and hangings, resulting in a richly coloured sitting room that is comfortable and welcoming.

Colourful comfort

This formal sitting room is given warmth and richness by the use of red on the walls and furnishings. Above the dado, the walls are papered with striped wallpaper in two tones of red, which are echoed in the paintwork on the cornice. The area below the dado has been marbled to compliment the magnificent fireplace. Subtle dragging on the bookcases either side of the fireplace helps these large items blend with the walls.

KEY TO THE TECHNIQUES

Frottage wall and door

The wall was painted with white **vinyl silk/satin latex** (see p. 72). An acrylic glaze in pale lilac was then applied and **frottaged** (see pp. 106–107) with sheets of newspaper.

The door, dado, and skirting/baseboard were painted in white **quick-drying/acrylic latex eggshell** (see p. 72). An acrylic glaze in raw umber was then applied and frottaged.

Colourwash wall with blue woodwork

The wall was painted with white **vinyl silk/satin latex** (see p. 72). It was then **colourwashed** (see pp. 82–83) with a yellow acrylic glaze and brushed out with a dry brush.

The shelf and skirting/baseboard were painted in a blue-grey **oil eggshell** (see p. 72).

Dragged trompe l'oeil panels

The wall was painted with white **vinyl silk/satin latex** (see p. 72). The **panels** (see p. 79) were then carefully measured and marked on the wall. They were painted to create a **trompe l'oeil** effect (see pp. 104–105) with blue and cream acrylic glazes.

The mitre lines for the **trompe l'oeil** effect (see pp. 104–105) were applied in grey matt emulsion/latex.

Frottage wall and door

Frottage ages a surface instantly, producing an irregular, slightly cracked appearance that has great depth and character. It looks wonderful and is extremely simple to do. Here, the combination of two subtle shades makes a pleasantly soothing colour scheme for a sitting room and the use of frottage on both walls and woodwork relates the two. Frottage is perfect for old walls that are naturally uneven; it also suits halls, staircases, and dining rooms.

Colourwash wall with blue woodwork

One of the simplest of all paint effects to achieve, colour-washing looks good in any room in the house. It makes an easy and relaxing backdrop for pictures, but it is equally successful left unadorned. The texture of the brushwork is unobtrusive and yet gives depth and shading to the wall. Here, the sunny yellow makes a warm, welcoming colour for a sitting room and it is set off by the rich blue wood-work and skirting/baseboard.

Dragged trompe l'oeil panels

These trompe l'oeil panels are most effective in a simple square or rectangular room with plain walls, rather than one with irregular recesses or sloping ceilings. This fairly complex technique produces a quiet, conservative look, particularly when carried out in soft colours. The panels create an atmosphere of ordered calm and can lend an ordi-nary room some importance. Trompe l'oeil panels would also make a restful look for a bedroom.

KEY TO THE TECHNIQUES

Subtle porphyry flick

The wall was painted in white **vinyl silk/satin latex** (see p. 72). A cream acrylic glaze was applied and **sponged** (see p. 87). Once this was dry, the wall was **flicked** (see p. 100) with concentrated glazes of raw umber and burnt sienna.

The door and skirting/baseboard were painted in off-white **oil eggshell** (see p. 72). The moulding was **picked out** (see p. 73) in terracotta glaze.

Chinese wallpaper

The wall was prepared and **wallpapered** (see pp. 114–119) in the usual way.

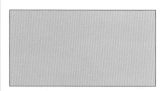

The area above the picture rail was painted in cream **matt emulsion/latex** (see p. 72).

The skirting/baseboard and picture rail were painted with burgundy **oil eggshell** (see p. 72).

Red ragging and black woodwork

The wall was painted in pale pink **vinyl silk/satin latex** (see p. 72). A red acrylic glaze was applied and **ragged**, then **softened** (see p. 86) with a badger brush.

The skirting/baseboard and **fireplace** (see p. 75) were painted in black matt emulsion/latex and given a coat of flat acrylic **varnish** (see p. 73).

Subtle porphyry flick

When used with such muted colours, this porphyry look is one of the most unobtrusive, yet pleasing of paint effects. It is undemanding on the eye but holds quiet interest when observed closely. Used in a sitting room, it is an easy finish to live with and provides a smart background for paintings and furniture. It would look its best in a room with generous proportions and plenty of natural light.

Chinese wallpaper

Oriental in style, this wallpaper has great charm with an almost fairytale quality. Despite the wealth of detail and busy figures, the subtle tones of colour keep the feeling serene. There is little space between the repeat design and the paper makes an effective backdrop for grand rooms and large classical paintings. Plain colour above the picture rail keeps the effect from being overwhelming and can help adjust the proportions of a tall room.

Red ragging and black woodwork

The glowing red sheen of the glazed walls combined with flat matt black of the skirting/baseboard and fireplace make an unusual and effective statement. It is a vibrant, daring mix, best suited to sitting rooms that are used mostly at night, where outrageous stories are exchanged and revolutions planned. Not a colour scheme for the faint-hearted, but certainly richly rewarding.

KEY TO THE TECHNIQUES

Yellow dragging in two tones

The wall was painted in white **vinyl silk/satin latex** (see p. 72). A yellow acrylic glaze was applied to the wall above the dado and **dragged** (see p. 84).

A deeper burnt yellow acrylic glaze was applied below the dado and **dragged** (see p. 84).

The woodwork was painted in white **quick-drying/acrylic latex eggshell** (see p. 72). Stone acrylic glaze was applied and **dragged** (see p. 84).

Sea-green colourwash and plastic bagging

The wall was painted in white **vinyl silk/satin latex** (see p. 72). A sea-green acrylic glaze was applied to the wall above the shelf and **plastic bagged** (see p. 87). A second layer was applied once the first was dry.

The same sea-green glaze was applied to the wall below the shelf and **colourwashed** (see pp. 82–83).

The shelf and skirting/base-board were painted with blue-grey **oil eggshell** (see p. 72).

Leaf stencil

The wall was painted with white **vinyl silk/satin latex** (see p. 72) and **ragged** (see p. 86) with acrylic glaze in soft beige. The **stencils** (see pp. 94–97) were applied with greenish grey matt emulsion/ latex. The centres were stippled lightly to add **3D texture** (see p. 97).

The woodwork was **dragged** (see p. 84) in beige glaze over quick-drying/acrylic eggshell.

Yellow dragging in two tones

Dragging is one of the most traditional paint effects. Its soft, subtle finish makes it a good background for prints and watercolours and it is an ideal effect for sitting rooms and bedrooms, where such pictures might be hung. The two tones of yellow look warm and friendly. The use of the darker yellow below the dado rail helps to ground the room and also helps to break up a tall wall in a room with a high ceiling.

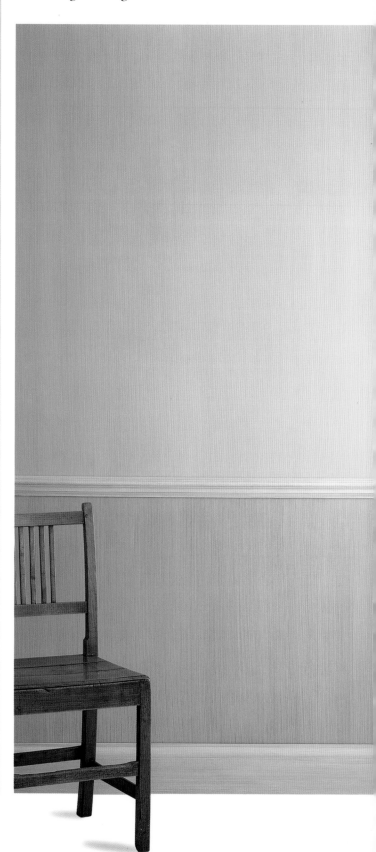

Sea-green colourwash and plastic bagging

Blues and greens are often thought of as cool colours, but this sea-green is rich and warm. The slightly lighter effect of the colourwashed area is a perfect foil for the denser, plastic-bagged effect above. Many people think they should use light colours in small rooms with little natural light, but I prefer to use strong, deep colours such as these to enrich the room and make it something special. The dark blue-grey woodwork enhances the rich colours.

Leaf stencil

The large scale of these stylized leaf stencils makes a bold effect and the regularity of the design is important to the finished look. The subdued colour scheme of subtle green on beige softens the design, and the shading within the stencils keeps the overall impression light and attractive. This treatment would suit a large, airy sitting room with plain, classic furnishings.

The Bathroom

A BATHROOM SHOULD BE a civilized, relaxing place, a haven from the frenetic pressures of life, where you ease into a world of steaming water, soothing lotions and warm fluffy towels. But all too often, the bathroom is squeezed into the smallest room in the house and feels mean and cramped. I would willingly sacrifice bedroom space to incorporate a generous bathroom, with room enough for a large bathtub, a sofa or comfortable chair, and shelves for books and magazines. The walls in such a bathroom might have a lick of deep-coloured paint, a special effect, or a rich wallpaper. A simpler bathroom with no clutter is ideal for a speedy invigorating shower. Tiles are a practical wall covering for such a room and can be highly decorative as well as easy to wipe clean.

Children's bathrooms should be colourful and fun to encourage unwilling bathers. Brightly coloured, tiled splashbacks and walls stencilled with animals or clowns are easy to do and always appealing.

Mosaic tiled bathroom
This bathroom has a cave-like look. The owners have decided to go with the darkness rather than try to counteract it and have used luscious dark blue tiling. The tiles inside the bathroom have a high gloss, giving them a mosaic-like look. This is increased by the tiny tiles edging the door and the skirting/baseboard area. The area around the door has been painted with a tile-like pattern and finished with gloss varnish.

Blue and white tiling

Clean, hygienic and uncluttered, this is an extremely practical bathroom. Everything can be wiped down and the tiled walls will come to no harm, no matter how deep and splashy your bath. The look is saved from being too clinical by the use of different designs of blue and white tiles. There is even chequerboard tiling around the mirror to add interest.

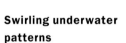

Swirling underwater patterns

This is a highly decorative and atmospheric bathroom with a feeling of fantasy in the richly coloured walls. Ceiling, cornice and walls have been treated with several layers of paint effect, creating swirling underwater patterns. You can imagine lying in the bath and feeling as though you are in the middle of the ocean. Fittings and woodwork are deliberately simple, allowing the rich paint effect to dominate.

KEY TO THE TECHNIQUES

Lime wallpaper and white tiles

The wall was **wallpapered** (see pp. 114–119) and given a coat of flat acrylic **varnish** (see p. 73). The woodwork was painted with white **oil eggshell** (see p. 72).

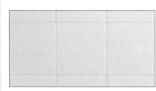

White **tiles** (see pp. 110–113) were applied to the wall beneath the dado.

Green walls with tortoiseshell band

The wall was painted with blue-green **vinyl silk/satin latex** (see p. 72).

The **dado** (see p. 78) was marked on the wall. The **tortoiseshell effect** (see p. 102) was applied with green and black acrylic glaze. The tramlines were stippled in **metallic gold** (see p. 71). The skirting/baseboard was prepared in quick-drying/acrylic latex eggshell and tortoiseshelled. The moulding was **picked out** (see p. 73) in **metallic gold**.

Trompe l'oeil leaves

The wall was painted with terracotta **matt emulsion/latex** (see p. 72).

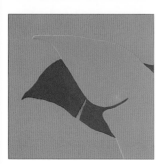

The leaves were drawn onto the wall and painted with two shades of green matt emulsion/latex, creating a **trompe l'oeil effect** (see pp. 104–105). The wall was **varnished** (see p. 73). The skirting/baseboard was painted in terracotta **oil eggshell** (see p. 72).

Lime wallpaper and white tiles

Plain white tiles combined with colourful patterned wallpaper gives a bright, attractive look, ideal for a bathroom used by children. The tiles provide an ample splashback area, reaching to well above the height of the average bath. The wallpaper can be given a coat of acrylic varnish so that it, too, is durable and easy to clean. Wallpaper is not the obvious choice for a bathroom, but when varnished and used with tiles it makes a refreshing change.

Green walls with tortoiseshell band

More adult in character, this wall treatment has a hint of decadence. Painting a room in such a deep, rich colour automatically creates a sumptuous, luxurious atmosphere. In this example, the richness of the green is enhanced by the gold-bordered tortoiseshell band and skirting/base-board. This look would also suit a dining room, particularly one that was used mostly in the evenings.

Trompe l'oeil leaves

Bold and arresting, this is an unusual look for a bathroom. The solid green palm leaves stand out against the rich terracotta base and there is no attempt to camouflage the stark white bathroom fittings. Leaves are among the easiest of all subjects to paint onto a wall, even for a beginner, and the infinite variety of leaf shapes that exist in nature allows plenty of scope.

KEY TO THE TECHNIQUES

Deep blue wallpaper

The picture rail and skirting/baseboard were painted in white **oil eggshell** (see p. 72). The wall above the picture rail was painted in white **vinyl silk/satin latex** (see p. 72).

The wall was prepared and **wallpapered** in the usual way (see pp. 114–119) and given a protective coat of flat acrylic **varnish** (see p. 73).

Crab and fish stencil

The wall above the dado was painted in yellow **matt emulsion/latex** (see p. 72).

The dado, wooden boarding, and skirting/baseboard were painted in pale grey **oil eggshell** (see p. 72).

The crab and fish motifs were **stencilled** (see pp. 94–97) in orange and blue matt emulsion/latex. A coat of flat **varnish** (see p. 73) was applied.

Wavy stripes

The wall was painted in white **matt emulsion/latex** (see p. 72). Guidelines for the **wavy stripes** (see p. 77) were drawn freehand so the effect was not too regimented, and alternate bands were painted in blue and green matt emulsion/latex. The wall was given a coat of flat acrylic **varnish** (see p. 73). The skirting/baseboard was painted in white **oil eggshell** (see p. 72).

Deep blue wallpaper

A bathroom should be a relaxing place, a haven where you retreat from the pressures of the world. This deep blue wallpaper is perfect for creating just such a soothing, restful atmosphere. Although the paper does feature a geometric design, it is subtle and unobtrusive. The white paint used on the skirting/baseboard, picture rail, and above provides a crisp, clean contrast to the deep blue and lifts the overall effect.

Crab and fish stencil

This design is both practical and attractive. The wooden boarding below the dado provides a useful splashback for the bath and basin, and the dado itself can be used as a narrow shelf for decorative items such as this starfish. The blue and yellow colour scheme has a genuine seaside look, which is echoed by the stencils. Fish and shellfish motifs like these have interesting shapes and always look appropriate in a bathroom.

Wavy stripes

Strong bands of colour make a bright, fun look for a bathroom, giving a feeling of being in the midst of the ocean. The blue, white, and green combination has a fresh, clean effect and, because the blue and green are similar in tone, they do not jar. Strongly contrasting colours used in such a way could be disruptive. This is an invigorating bathroom, more suitable for a speedy, dynamic shower than a long relaxing bath.

The Bedroom

MOST ADULTS want a bedroom that is a serene, restful space, with colours and effects that are kind to the senses. Bedrooms are personal retreats, places where you can relax and be yourself.

For some, a simple bedroom is best. A small room with enough space for a comfortable bed, table, and reading light is enough. The look can be softened with a few pictures on the walls, a small mirror, and a bedcover and curtains in a beautiful fabric.

Large, elegant bedrooms can be charming, too. They do not have to withstand the wear and tear of a kitchen or sitting room so you can happily choose pale shades and

delicate designs. Warm, parchment-coloured walls are popular as are gentle antique whites, delicate yellows, or the softness of cornflower or duck egg blues. Fabric-covered walls look soft and comforting and muffle sound. Camouflage bulky built-in cupboards by painting them the same colour as the walls. Children's bedrooms should also be havens but you may want to make them bright and cheerful by painting walls with colourful, invigorating stripes or entertaining stencil designs.

The right lighting is crucial. In general, keep the main source of light subdued, but make sure that you have a good strong reading light by the bed.

Fabric walls, above

The fabric-covered walls in this bedroom create a comfortable atmosphere. Fabric absorbs sound and so helps make a bedroom a haven of
peace. The blue-grey colour scheme is tranquil and harmonious and
perfectly set off by the white woodwork and cornice. This is strictly a
room for adults – any dirty fingerprints cannot be wiped away.

Harlequin stencilling, left

A geometric stencil design was a bold choice for an irregular shaped
room like this but works surprisingly well. The colours are warm and rich
and help to create a cosy welcoming atmosphere. The ceiling is painted
the same colour as the background behind the stencils and a paint
effect has been applied.

Tartan bedroom, right

Instead of covering walls with fabric, paint them to look like fabric. The
tartan effect used below the dado level here is colourful and fun. It is
deliberately left quite irregular, with wobbly lines to echo the fluidity of
material. Yellow walls pick up the yellow used in the tartan.

KEY TO THE TECHNIQUES

Yellow frottage

The wall was painted in white **vinyl silk/satin latex** (see p. 72). A yellow acrylic glaze was applied to the wall above the dado and **frottaged** (see pp. 106–107) with newspaper.

The wall below the dado was **sponged** (see p. 87) in the same yellow acrylic glaze.

The woodwork was **dragged** (see p. 84) in acrylic yellow glaze applied over white quick-drying/acrylic latex eggshell.

Foam roller stripes

The wall was first painted in pale blue **matt emulsion/latex** (see p. 72). Stripes were applied with specially cut **foam rollers** (see pp. 90–91), using yellow, lilac, and deep violet matt emulsion/latex. The skirting/baseboard was painted in yellow **oil eggshell** (see p. 72).

Giraffe stencil

The wall above the dado was painted in pale yellow **matt emulsion/latex** (see p. 72). The giraffe and dragonfly **stencils** (see pp. 94–97) were applied in suitable emulsion/latex colours.

The wall below the dado was painted in strong yellow **matt emulsion/latex** (see p. 72).

The skirting/baseboard and dado rail were painted in dark blue **oil eggshell** (see p. 72).

Yellow frottage

Frottaged yellow walls have a soft 'undecorated' look. The random nature of the technique makes the walls look pleasantly aged yet elegant, in the manner of a crumbling Italian palazzo. When carried out in gentle, unthreatening colours, frottage has an extremely restful appearance and is well suited to bedrooms. The sponged area below the dado steadies and compliments the frottage.

Foam roller stripes

Multi-coloured stripes are surprisingly easy to achieve and bring a feeling of vigour and energy to a room. Fun and visually stimulating, this is a perfect treatment for a child's bedroom, but would also be enjoyed by many adults. The pale blue, lilac, and violet tone well together, while the yellow provides a vibrant note that enlivens the colour scheme. Stripes are practical too – few scratches and dirty fingermarks would be visible on these walls.

Giraffe stencil

This is a striking and original effect for a young child's bedroom. Animal motifs are always popular and giraffes have a particularly appealing graphic shape. The fluttering dragonflies break up the more formal pattern of the paired animals and add interest to the design. The sunny background yellows and the blue on the skirting/baseboard and dado increase the bright, stimulating atmosphere created by the stencilled walls.

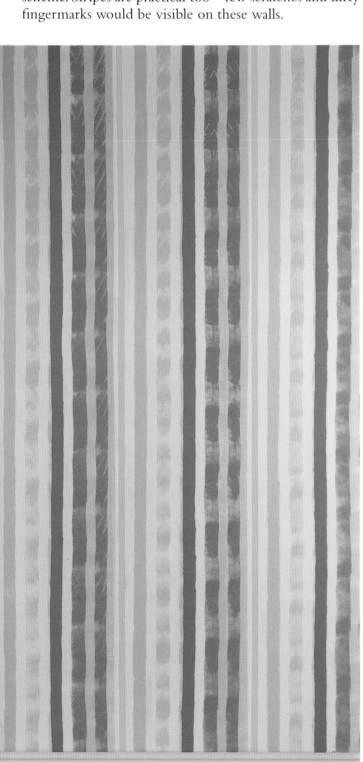

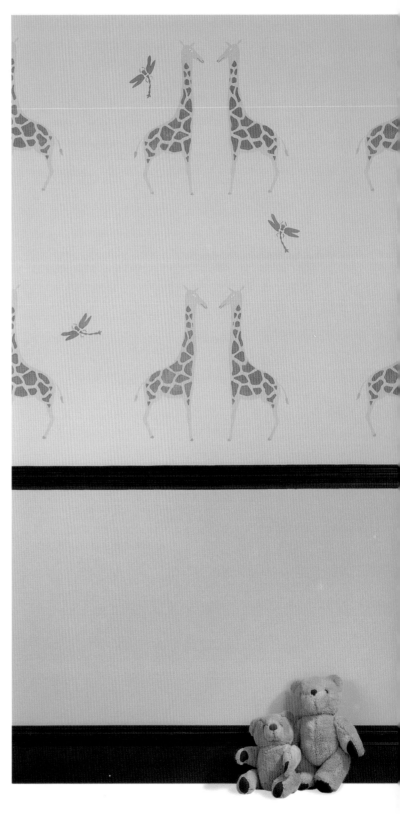

KEY TO THE TECHNIQUES

Damask stencil

The wall was painted in white **vinyl silk/satin latex** (see p. 72) and **ragged** (see p. 86) in an acrylic glaze of ochre and umber. It was then **stencilled** (see pp. 94–97) with an acrylic glaze in burnt sienna. The skirting/baseboard was painted in white **oil eggshell** (see p. 72).

Fabric panel

The wall was painted in pale cream **matt emulsion/latex** (see p. 72). The woodwork was painted in cream **oil eggshell** (see p. 72).

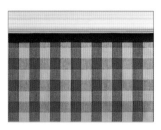

To make the **fabric panel** (see pp. 120–121), a wooden frame was attached to the wall under the dado. Wadding and fabric were stapled to the frame. Ribbon was glued to the fabric top and bottom to hide staples.

Flower border stencil on ragged wall

The wall was painted in white **vinyl silk/satin latex** (see p.72) and then **ragged** (see p. 86) with an acrylic glaze of soft pink.

The flower border was **stencilled** (see pp. 94–97) across the top of the wall in a deep pink acrylic glaze. A slightly deeper mix was used for the berries and the shading on the bows.

The skirting/baseboard was painted in white **quick-drying/acrylic latex eggshell** (see p. 72) and **dragged** (see p. 84) with the pink glaze.

Damask stencil

This all-over stencil design looks like wallpaper, but, providing you do it yourself, is a much cheaper way of treating your walls. Although the design is intricate, its regularity and harmonious colour scheme make it calm and pleasing to the eye. Such a large design looks most effective in a large room; it could overwhelm a small space. This traditional stencilled look is also suitable for a hall or dining room, and for both town and country houses.

Fabric panel

Mixing plain cream emulsion/latex paint and fresh blue and white check fabric creates a soothing, Scandinavian look for this room. The bold check is balanced by the larger expanse of restful cream above it and the two horizontal lines of dark ribbon provide a steadying accent. The soft texture of the fabric, padded by the cotton wadding beneath it, brings a feeling of luxurious comfort, ideally suited to a bedroom.

Flower border stencil on ragged wall

The combination of the subtle ragging and floral stencil design makes this a very delicate, feminine look, perfect for a comfortable bedroom. The border adds interest and individuality, but it does not intrude on the room. This style of stencilling suits a fairly conventional setting and is best used on walls without cornices. The delicacy of this stencil design suits soft warm colours.

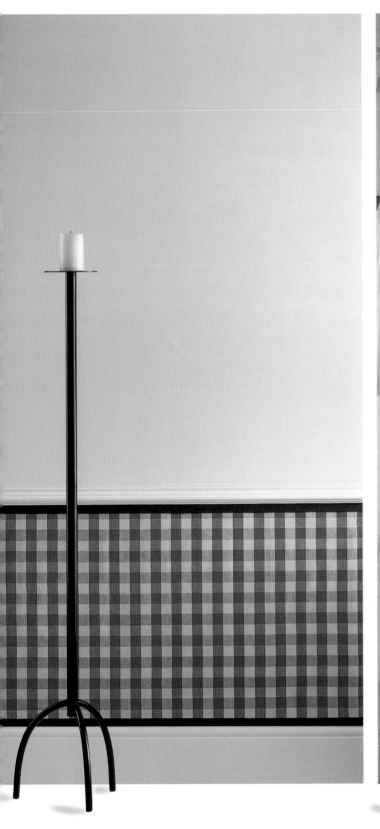
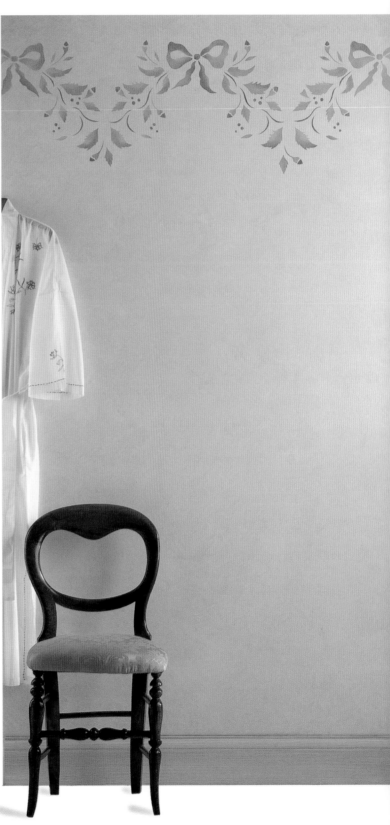

Basic Techniques

Equipment

YOUR BRUSHES and other decorating equipment are items to be treasured and enjoyed. You don't have to possess every one of the items shown on these pages, but you do need the right tools for the job if you are to get good results. Think about what you will want before you start decorating and gather everything together. There is nothing worse than being half way through a job and finding that you need more masking tape or a smaller brush. Keeping your equipment organized and orderly is a fundamental part of decorating.

Brushes

Basic brushes

Buy good quality brushes – they will last longer and shed fewer hairs as you work. At the very least, you will need a 10cm (4in) brush for applying paint to walls and a 2.5cm (1in) brush for working on smaller areas such as skirting/baseboards.

2.5cm (1in) brush for painting small areas and stippling small stencils

10cm (4in) brush for applying emulsion/latex

15cm (6in) brush for colourwashing and laying on glaze

Specialist brushes

If you are going to try special techniques, such as woodgraining or paint effects, you will need the right brush for the job.

Hoghair mottler for woodgraining

15cm (6in) brush for dragging

Horsehair flogging brush used in woodgraining

Badger brush for softening colourwashes and other paint effects

Gliders

Gliding brushes were originally designed for applying varnish. They are soft and controllable, and they do not shed their hair as easily as many other cheaper brushes. I like to use them for things other than varnishing. They are ideal, for example, for dragging small areas such as doors and architraves.

10cm (4in) glider

7.5cm (3in) glider

6cm (2½in) glider

5cm (2in) glider

Stippling brushes

Pure bristle stippling brushes are available in a variety of sizes from 10 x 2.5cm (4 x 1in) to 23 x 18cm (9 x 7in). The larger the area you are stippling, the larger the brush you will need. Circular stippling brushes are ideal for filling in awkward corners and edges.

Large stippling brush with handle for stippling walls

Smaller stippling brush with handle for stippling skirting/baseboards and other small areas

Circular stippling brush for corners and edges

Useful extras

Although not essential, other types of brush, such as fitches, stencil brushes, and artist's brushes, are useful for special details or for reaching into awkward corners.

Stencil brush for stippling large stencils

Angled fitch for reaching into awkward corners

Pointed fitch for detailed work such as applying paint to moulding on a skirting/baseboard or cornice

Artist's brush for adding small details

CLEANING BRUSHES

Look after your brushes and they will last much longer

Good brushes are not cheap, but if given tender loving care they will last and give excellent service. Acrylic glazes and paints dry quickly, so clean your brushes as soon as possible after use. Dunk the brush into warm water and liquid detergent when you have finished painting. Then take a wire brush and brush firmly through the bristles to remove any paint that remains (left). If brushes are left dirty and the paint dries hard, try softening them with methylated spirits before combing the bristles through with a wire brush as before and washing in warm water and mild detergent. Stippling brushes and soft-haired badger brushes need particular care and should never be left to dry without washing. If you use oil-based paint, clean brushes with white spirit followed by warm water and mild detergent. And don't forget to wash out your paint kettles, leaving them ready for next time.

Basic painting equipment

When painting with brushes, decant your paint into a kettle. If working with rollers you will need paint trays. Always have a roll of mutton cloth for wiping brushes, cleaning off excess paint and a million other jobs.

Mask for protection
from fumes when
painting

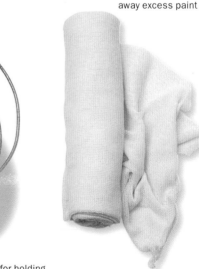

Pads for
mask

Mutton cloth for wiping
brushes and cleaning
away excess paint

Paint tray and
foam roller

Kettles for holding
paint when working
with brushes

Preparation equipment

Basics for preparing any surface include steel wool, a selection of sandpapers, and a filling knife and filler. Depending on the surface you are working on, you may need special items, such as an electric stripper for removing old wallpaper. Other useful equipment includes a ladder and dust sheets to cover floor and furniture.

Steel wool for rubbing down rough areas

Sandpaper for sanding down filler

Dusting brush for sweeping surfaces free of dust before painting

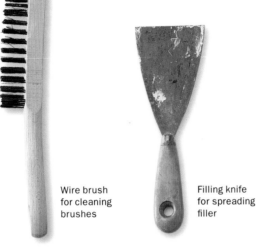

Wire brush for cleaning brushes

Filling knife for spreading filler

Filler for repairing cracks and holes in walls

Measuring and cutting equipment

You will need a good steel ruler and a plumb line for marking vertical lines on the wall for stripes and positioning wallpaper. Have a pencil handy, too. Sharp scissors and a craft knife are essential for such techniques as stencilling, découpage, and wallpapering. Have plenty of masking tape for marking up stripes or edges – low-tack tape is best.

Spirit level for checking that lines are straight

Low-tack masking tape for marking stripes and masking lines

Pencil

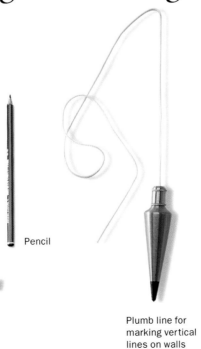

Plumb line for marking vertical lines on walls

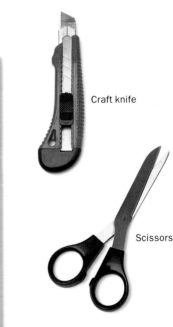

Craft knife

Scissors

Steel ruler

Paint

THE SIMPLEST WAY to paint a room is with beautiful, uncomplicated emulsion/latex. Water-based, quick-drying and virtually odourless, it is a joy to apply. Matt emulsion/latex has a high chalk content and its consequent lack of shine makes it an excellent choice for uneven walls. Any marks or scuffs that occur are easy to re-touch. Vinyl silk emulsion/satin latex has a slight sheen and so is easier to wipe clean. Since it is not porous, it makes the perfect base for acrylic glazes. An acrylic glaze is a water-based, colourless medium to which you add acrylic pigment from tubes and water. This translucent solution is used for paint effects and for faux and antique finishes.

TYPES OF PAINT USED IN STYLE DIRECTORY

Matt emulsion/latex

A water-based paint with a dead flat, chalky finish, this is most suitable for walls and ceilings. Easy to apply, matt emulsion/latex has no noxious fumes.

Vinyl silk/satin latex

A water-based paint with a mid-sheen and a silky finish. It is suitable for wall areas that need frequent wiping and for use as a base for acrylic glazes.

Quick-drying/ acrylic latex eggshell

A water-based paint with a mid-sheen finish, this is suitable for woodwork and for use as a base for acrylic glazes.

Oil eggshell

An oil-based paint with a mid-sheen finish. Suitable for woodwork, it is tougher and more durable than water-based eggshell.

Mixing a glaze

A glaze is mixed with water and pigment colours. I always use at least three colours in a glaze and sometimes as many as six. It is hard to give exact instructions – you have to experiment to get the colour you want. Always add small amounts of colour and test before adding any more. Be particularly careful with black and remember that you can always add more black to a mixture, but you can't take it away. With other colours you can reduce the effect more easily by adding glaze and water.

1 Pour some acrylic glaze and water into a paint kettle. The mix should be about 75 per cent glaze and 25 per cent water.

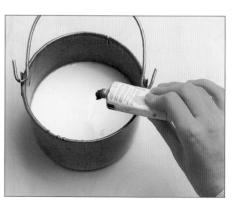

2 Start adding the first pigment, a little at a time. This warm terracotta is mixed with burnt sienna, cadmium red, and raw sienna.

3 Stir the mixture thoroughly to work the pigment into the glaze.

4 Add the other pigments and stir again briskly. Begin testing the colour on the wall, adding more pigment, a little at a time, if the colour is too light. If it gets too dark, add more glaze and water.

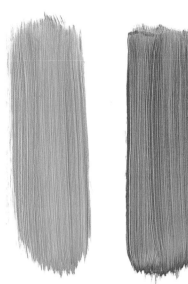

Finished glazes

These swatches show three variations of this glaze, any of which could be used. You may be happy with the lightest version. If not, add more pigment to achieve a richer effect.

Mixing gold paint

Small amounts of metallic paint look wonderful and add glamour and excitement to a room. Use them to pick out the moulding on a skirting/baseboard or to add details to a stencil, for example. To mix a metallic gold, you need some bronze powder in rich pale gold, button polish, and methylated spirits.

1 Put a couple of spoonfuls of bronze powder and button polish in a small dish.

2 Pour some methylated spirits into another dish. Take a small brush and start to mix the button polish and powder together, then dip the brush into the methylated spirits.

3 Continue mixing the paint, taking the brush back and forth between the methylated spirits and the mixture. The methylated spirits lubricates the mixture, but you only need a small amount.

4 When the button polish and powder are thoroughly amalgamated, the paint is ready to use. Clean the brush thoroughly with methylated spirits to remove the gold paint.

Applying Paint and Varnish

I PREFER TO APPLY PAINT with a brush and only use a roller for ceilings or special stripe effects. A roller often produces a grainy, orange-peel look which spoils the look of a room. You achieve a superior finish with a brush and it does not take much longer. Whether using a roller or a brush, it helps to dilute emulsion/latex with water (10 per cent water to 90 per cent emulsion) to make it spread more easily – particularly for the first coat. Varnish must be applied with even more care than paint. If coverage is uneven it will look a mess.

Emulsion/latex

Always use a paint kettle and transfer paint to it a little at a time. The kettle is lighter to carry than a whole can of paint and there is not such a disaster if you drop it. Stir the paint before transferring it to the kettle. Never overload your brush. Using more paint does not make for quicker painting but for walls emblazoned with agricultural furrows and drips.

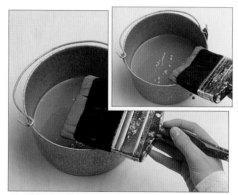

1 Pour some emulsion/latex into your paint kettle. Dip the end of the brush into the paint and wipe off any excess on the side of the kettle (see inset).

2 Start at the top right corner of the wall. Lay the paint on with even criss-crossing strokes.

3 Once the first coat is complete, begin applying a second coat. Make sure that you cover the whole area – this is harder when working with colour onto colour than when working onto undercoat.

Eggshell

Before painting raw wooden skirting/baseboards, doors, or other woodwork, first apply a suitable primer, rub down and fill where necessary. Apply an undercoat and rub down again. Finally, apply two coats of eggshell. Two coats of quick-drying/acrylic latex eggshell can be applied in a day, but if using oil-based eggshell, leave 24 hours between coats.

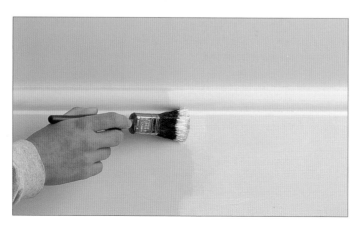

Take a 2.5cm (1in) brush and apply the first coat of eggshell to the skirting/baseboard. Work back and forth in small stages. Apply a second coat of eggshell in the same way.

Picking out mouldings

First remove
the finger and
Simply painti
straightforwa
ing the panel
and then wor
rails, starting
door. Be care
not collect in
mouldings an

If you want t
the door, mal
stop and start
tions of the s
reflect the co
door. Leave tl
last. The dott
diagram show
break points l
with oil eggsl
ing/acrylic la
are going to ;

Add interest to a skirting/baseboard, door, or cornice by
picking out the moulding in a contrasting glaze or even in
metallic paint. Carefully mask the area with tape before painting. Don't overdo this kind of detailing – a small amount is
effective; too much can look overwhelming.

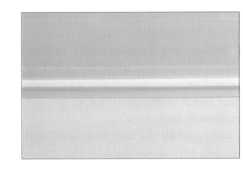

1 Paint the skirt-
ing/baseboard
with eggshell. Apply
low-tack masking
tape just above and
just below the bulge
of the moulding.

2 Using glaze or
metallic paint
and a 2.5cm (1in)
brush, apply paint
to the strip between
the tapes. Use a dry
brush so the paint
does not bleed under
the tape.

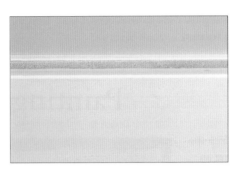

3 Carefully remove
both tapes to
reveal the painted
detail.

Varnish

Always work
to the outside
a fireplace, w
simply painti
an acrylic gla
effect. Use oi
quick-drying
eggshell if yo
apply glaze. A
you want a m
place, use em
then varnish

Three types of acrylic varnish are available
– flat, satin, which has a slight sheen, and
gloss, with a definite shine. Always stir
the varnish really thoroughly in the can
before you start or you may not get
the intended finish. Varnish needs to be
applied with great care. You must make
sure every part of the area is evenly
covered with the same amount of varnish
– one reason why two coats are generally
recommended. Use a 5cm (2in) gliding
brush to apply varnish.

1 Pour some varnish into a paint kettle and
stir it carefully once more.

2 Apply the first coat of varnish with a 5cm
(2in) gliding brush. Make sure the surface
is completely covered.

3 Take some wet
and dry sand-
piper and fill a paint
kettle with cold water.
Submerge the sand-
paper in water then
very gently rub over
the varnished wall
with small circular
movements. Apply
a second coat.

Finished effect
Going over the wall
with wet and dry
sandpaper between
coats gives a better
finish. If you lift any
paint with the sand-
paper, re-touch with
the wall colour before
applying the second
coat of varnish.

Measuring and Masking

FOR SPECIAL TECHNIQUES, such as stripes, tartan, stencilling, découpage, and fake blocks, the design must first be worked out, then measured and marked on the walls to be decorated. Tempting though it may be just to start and hope for the best, time spent working out the design properly is never wasted. But don't panic if your last stripe is a few centimetres short or your stencil frieze doesn't join exactly – no one but you is likely to notice such minor imperfections. Faultless, perfectly striped or stencilled rooms can often lack character.

Remember that few rooms have precise measurements so you will have to adjust slightly here and there to allow for variations in the depth of a skirting/baseboard or the height of a ceiling. More informal designs are often better placed by eye, instead of being painstakingly measured and marked. The results can look refreshingly natural and unsophisticated.

Always use low-tack masking tape when marking stripes or dado borders or you risk pulling away paint with the tape when you remove it.

Measuring for stripes

Stripes are easy to do if properly measured and marked. First decide on the width of the stripe – a wide stripe might be 23 or 25cm (9 or 10in). Do a rough check that this fits the room by measuring round the skirting/baseboard (see p. 88) and adjust if necessary. Then mark the stripes on the walls.

1 Decide which is the most prominent wall in the room – the one that will be looked at most. Measure and mark the centre of the wall with a pencil.

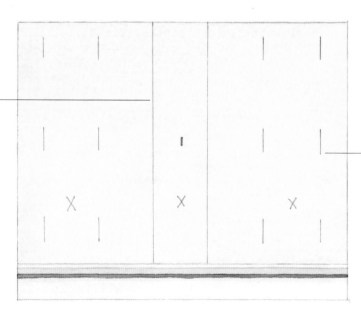

2 The first mark is the mid-point of the central stripe on the wall. If the stripes are to be 23cm (9in) wide, measure and mark 11.5 cm (4½in) to either side of the central mark.

3 Measure and mark each side of this stripe at points up and down the wall.

4 With a ruler or straight edge, join up the points with faint pencil lines so the full extent of the stripe is marked.

5 Working from the edge of the central stripe, continue measuring and marking 23cm (9in) stripes around the room, allowing them to go round corners where necessary. Mark every other stripe with a light cross.

6 Apply low-tack masking tape to either side of the central stripe. The tape should be to the outside of the pencil lines. Continue taping up every other stripe in this way.

7 Apply your chosen paint or glaze to the taped up stripes, marked with a cross. Remove the cross first.

8 As each stripe is completed, carefully remove the masking tape from both sides. Check that the paint has not bled underneath the tape.

Working round obstacles

In every room stripes will meet windows, doors, and other obstacles. Don't worry about these. Just let the stripes continue as they fall. The finished effect will look all the more natural.

Wavy stripes

Not all designs need to be measured and marked. Some look best drawn freehand, with any variations and inaccuracies making part of the charm. These wavy stripes should be approximately the same width, but they don't have to be perfectly even to look good. Be brave and trust your eye.

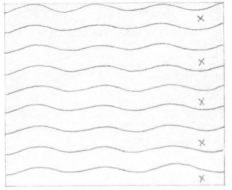

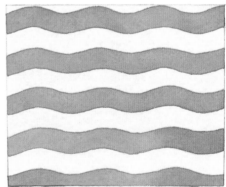

1 Paint the whole wall with vinyl silk/satin latex in the lighter of the two shades to be used. Take a pencil and a deep breath and draw wavy lines across the wall approximately 30cm (12in) apart.

2 Using a 2.5cm (1in) brush, carefully cut into the top wavy line with the darker colour. Keep the edge crisp and fill the stripe as shown. Repeat with alternate waves. Waves can be painted different colours (see p. 56).

Measuring for a false dado or border

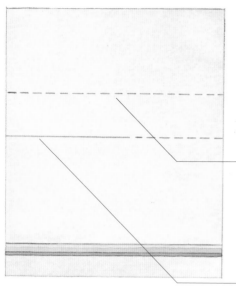

1 Decide on the position of the dado or border, usually 76–90cm (30–36in) above the skirting/baseboard. Measure and mark the top and bottom of the dado or border.

2 Measure and mark at intervals around the room. Join up the marks to make two parallel lines marking the dado.

3 Apply low-tack masking tape along the outer edges of both lines. Paint as desired then remove the masking tape carefully. Apply fresh masking tape for each layer of paint for a crisp line.

Measuring for marble blocks

Make sure that the size of the blocks is related to the size of the wall or room. For a wall that is 2.5m (8ft) high, for example, blocks of 30cm (12in) deep and 50cm (20in) across look good. The higher the room, the larger the blocks should be.

1 For a 2.5m (8ft) wall, divide the wall into equal 30cm (12in) spaces and mark with pencil as shown. Make several marks across the wall.

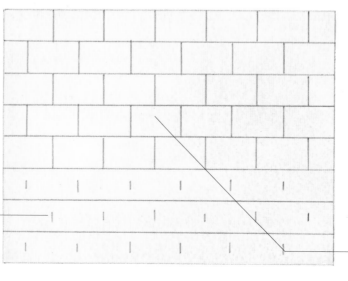

2 Using the marks as a guide, draw horizontal lines right across the wall with a straight edge or ruler.

3 Starting from the top right corner of the wall, mark the width of the blocks at 50cm (20in) intervals. It doesn't matter if some blocks are slightly smaller – it can even make the effect look more natural.

4 Draw in the vertical lines for the top row of blocks with a ruler or straight edge. Use this as a guide for the remaining blocks. The second line should be staggered as shown, so start with a half block. The third line should be the same as the first, and so on.

Measuring for trompe l'oeil panels

Trompe l'oeil panels can be made on walls or flat doors. A long wall looks best broken up into a large central panel with two smaller ones on either side. On a shorter wall, make two panels of equal size. A small space looks best with just one. A small panel is also a useful way of treating the area above a door. The diagrams here show how to measure for one large panel and two smaller panels on a wall below the dado.

1 Measure and mark with pencil 10cm (4in) down from the dado, up from the skirting/baseboard and in from the sides. These will be the stile areas.

2 Using a long ruler or straight edge, join up all the marks to create a long panel, with a 10cm (4in) stile surrounding it.

3 Measure and mark the central point of the panel. The smaller panels should be approximately half the size of the central panel. Work out the size of your central panel accordingly and mark its outside edges as shown. Measure and mark 10cm (4in) beyond these points for the vertical stiles between the panels.

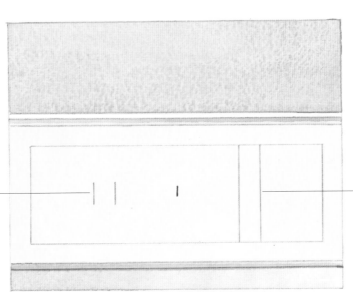

4 Draw in the vertical lines to create the three panels and the vertical stiles that divide them.

5 Remove the pencil mark at the centre of the panel and the horizontal pencil marks across the stile as shown. (See pp. 104–105 for information on painting trompe l'oeil panels.)

Special Techniques

Paint Effects

THERE ARE TWO TYPES of paint effects included here. In the first group, an acrylic glaze is applied to a wall prepared with vinyl silk emulsion/satin latex. The glaze is then moved around or lifted with a variety of tools, depending on the effect desired. It can be brushed out with a colourwashing brush, lifted with a sponge, rag, or plastic bag, stippled with a stippling brush, or dragged. In the second group, matt emulsion/latex is applied with a brush or roller in bold stripes or tartan designs.

Acrylic glazes have a wonderful translucent look. They give an instant three-dimensional quality that creates depth and atmosphere in a room. The colour, which is mixed with glaze and acrylic pigments and diluted with water (see p. 70), can be as rich or subtle as you want it to be. The simplest of the effects described here is probably colour-washing, which is easy to do and looks good even on lumpy walls. Ragging, plastic bagging, and sponging take a little more practice but are quite simple and suited to most surfaces. Dragging and stippling need more care and dragging is only really effective on a flat, even surface.

Striped effects

I paint bold, striped effects in two ways, both using matt emulsion/latex. Paint simple wide stripes with a brush, remembering to measure and mask carefully first (see pp. 76–77). To make the stripes more interesting, apply an effect, such as ragging, as well. Ribbon-like stripes are easy to paint with a roller. Cut the foam of the roller into raised bands to make the stripes.

Sunny yellow colourwash

Simple, yet stunning, colourwashing looks good in any home. The marks of the criss-crossing brush strokes add texture and and depth, creating an effect that is interesting and unpretentious.

Colourwashing

Colourwashing creates a soft, weathered look, ideal for concealing uneven walls. The wall is first covered with a coat of vinyl silk/satin latex. You add an acrylic glaze (see p. 70) with sweeping, criss-crossing strokes, and then brush out the colour while it is still wet with a dry brush. For a deeper effect, apply a second coat of glaze. You will need a 15cm (6in) brush for laying on the glaze and a dry 15cm (6in) brush for brushing the colour out (see p. 66).

Green
acrylic glaze

1 Paint the wall with white vinyl silk/satin latex (see p. 72). Starting in the top right-hand corner, apply glaze to an area about 90cm (36in) square, using sweeping, criss-cross strokes. Take the brush down from the right to the left and turn it over and move from the left down to the right (see inset) with a flowing motion.

2 Take a dry 15cm (6in) brush and go over the area you have glazed brushing out the colour, again using criss-cross strokes. For a fairly coarse colourwash, press quite hard with the stock of the brush so that it leaves its impression. Brush first one way then the other.

3 As you work, the colourwashing brush will pick up paint. Keep a rag handy and wipe excess paint off the tips of the brush between sections. You will find you have to wipe the brush more and more often as it gets wetter.

4 Using the laying-on brush, apply glaze to the next section of the wall (see p. 74 for information on how to glaze a wall in sections). Make sure that this section is carefully blended with the one before, leaving no white areas or hard lines.

5 Using the dry brush, soften the glaze in the same way as before, with criss-cross stokes. Continue Steps 1–5 until the whole wall is colourwashed.

Finished effect

The uneven finish and brush strokes of colourwashing make this a relaxed effect, suitable for all but the most formal rooms. For this fairly coarse colourwash, you press quite hard with the brush so the stock leaves a definite impression.

A SOFTER GLAZE

Colourwashing can be as pronounced or subtle as you like, depending on how you use the brush

For a softer, more subtle effect, use the tip of the colourwashing brush only, so the stock makes less impression on the glaze (see below).

Dragging

Dragging is a most traditional effect, not suited to uneven walls. Prepare the wall with vinyl silk/satin latex and apply a glaze (see p. 70). Using a dragging brush (see p. 66), you drag down the wet glaze, making lines of bristle marks.

Pale blue
acrylic glaze

1 First prepare and paint the wall with white vinyl silk/satin latex (see p. 72). Using a 15cm (6in) laying-on brush, lay a strip of glaze about 40cm (15in) wide from the top right-hand corner to the bottom of the wall. Work as smoothly and evenly as possible.

2 Take a dry 15cm (6in) dragging brush and gently drag the glaze down the wall in one smooth unbroken movement. Take the brush back to the top and drag the next part of the strip, allowing the brush to overlap the first dragged section slightly.

3 As you work, glaze will collect above the skirting/baseboard. When the first strip is completed, wipe the tip of the brush with a rag (see inset). Place the brush at an angle so the tips are tucked into the top of the skirting/baseboard and flick the brush up to work in the excess paint and give a neat finish. Wipe any glaze off the skirting/baseboard.

4 Lay a second strip of the blue glaze from the top to the bottom of the wall as in Step 1. Overlap this slightly with the first strip so that the two blend together well.

5 Drag the second strip as in Step 2, being careful to wipe the brush and flick it up above the skirting/baseboard as before. Continue until the whole wall is dragged.

Final effect

For a softer look (far left), keep a light hand with the dragging brush so that the lines are not too evident. For a stronger effect (left), hold the brush more firmly and apply more pressure as you drag. If lines look wobbly, re-drag immediately, before the glaze has time to dry, to straighten them. After dragging you may need to re-touch the ceiling and skirting/baseboard if you get glaze on them.

Stippling

Stippling is a flat, delicate effect. Apply glaze (see p. 70) to a wall painted with vinyl silk/satin latex and then go over it with a stippling brush to lift paint and break up the colour. You will need a stippling brush of an appropriate size (see p. 67). Use a small brush to stipple corners and any other areas that are awkward to reach with the large stippling brush.

Yellow acrylic glaze

1 First prepare the wall and paint with white vinyl silk/satin latex (see p. 72). Using a large laying-on brush, apply the glaze to an area of about 50cm (20in) square at the top right-hand corner of the wall.

2 Take a stippling brush (see inset). Holding the brush at right angles to the wall, move systematically over the area, punching firmly onto the glaze. The bristle tips leave lots of tiny imprints.

3 Avoid making lines with the stippling brush. If you do make a horizontal line, go over it with a vertical line of stippling and vice versa. Use a small brush to stipple corners and awkward edges. Continue applying glaze and stippling until the wall is complete.

Final effect
Stippling softens and gives subtle interest to an area of flat colour. For the effect to look its best, keep up a firm steady motion to produce stippling that is even and consistent.

VARIATION

A darker glaze requires more robust action with the stippling brush, but the effect is rich and textural. Here, some flicking (see p. 100) has been added to the stipple.

Ragging

Ragging is a simple but effective technique. You apply a coloured glaze (see p. 70) to a prepared wall a section at a time (see p. 74), then go over it with a piece of crumpled mutton cloth, lifting the wet paint. It can be as soft or pronounced as you wish. You need a badger brush (see p. 66) for softening.

Terracotta acrylic glaze

1 First prepare the wall and paint with white vinyl silk/satin latex (see p. 72). Mix the glaze and apply to an area of about 90cm (36in) square at the top right-hand corner of the wall. Use rough criss-crossing strokes (see p. 82).

2 Cut a piece of mutton cloth or other plain rag about 30cm (12in) long and hold it bunched in the hand as shown above, so that folds form on the surface.

3 Gently dab all over the glazed area with the bunched rag. Use gentle movements – there is no need to thump at the wall. Continue to glaze and rag sections until the wall is complete, taking a fresh rag from time to time.

4 Using a small brush, gently stipple corners and areas above the skirting/baseboard which would be difficult to rag neatly. Hold the brush at right angles to the wall.

Final effect

The completed wall has subtle variations of colour and texture. Ragging can also be used in combination with other techniques such as stencilling and wide stripes.

SOFTENED RAGGING

To create a more subtle effect, gently brush over the ragged glaze with a badger brush to soften the markings of the rag

Apply the glaze and rag. Take a badger brush and stroke the surface of the ragged glaze in different directions.

The badger brush softens and blends the imprint of the rag, creating a quieter, more subtle effect with added depth.

Plastic bagging

Plastic bagging is done in exactly the same way as ragging, but using an ordinary plastic bag instead of a soft cloth. Since the bag is not absorbent, it will leave a harsher, crisper effect than the rag.

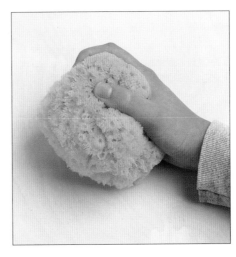

1 First prepare the wall and apply the glaze as for ragging (Step 1). Crumple an ordinary plastic bag in your hand and dab all over the glazed area, lifting the wet glaze.

Finished effect
Plastic bagging creates a more pronounced and coarser effect than sponging and ragging and is ideal for lumpy walls.

Sponging

Easy to do, sponging is similar to ragging. You prepare the wall as usual and apply glaze. You then go over the wall, lifting the wet glaze with a large, slightly damp natural sponge. The effect can be soft or more pronounced depending on how firmly you apply the sponge.

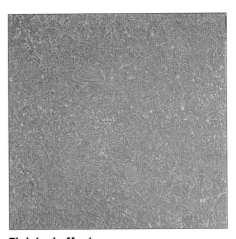

1 You will need a large damp natural sponge. One that has been well-used and softened will do the job better than a brand new sponge.

2 First paint the wall with white vinyl silk/satin latex (see p. 72). Apply glaze as for ragging (Step 1). Take the sponge and dab all over the glazed area, being careful not to remove too much paint. Stipple awkward corners (see Step 4, p. 86).

Finished effect
Simple but effective, sponging makes an attractive finish on its own or can form the background to a more elaborate effect such as stencilling.

Wide stripes

Wide stripes like these can be as subtle or bold as you want. First, you paint the wall all over in the lighter colour. Then you decide on the width of your stripes and measure and mark up the wall accordingly (see p. 76). You then paint alternate stripes in a darker colour. You will need a 10cm (4in) brush (see p. 66).

Blue matt emulsion/latex

Lilac matt emulsion/latex

MARKING OUT THE STRIPES

It is essential to measure out the stripes around the skirting/baseboard of your wall before starting, to check that they are going to fit neatly.

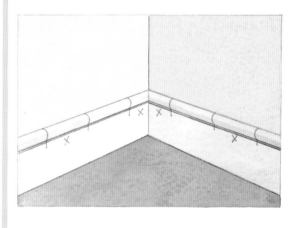

Decide on the width of your stripes – the stripes here are 23cm (9in). Measure the skirting/baseboard to check that your chosen width of stripe fits the wall neatly. If not, you can change the width of stripe accordingly or allow a stripe to go round a corner. See p. 76 for more information on measuring and marking stripes.

1 First prepare the wall and paint with violet matt emulsion/latex (see p. 72). Measure and mark the positions of the stripes in pencil across the width of the wall (see p. 76).

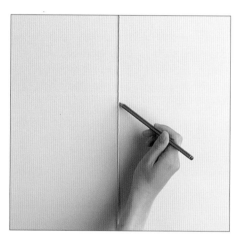

2 Using a plumb line – you can make one with a piece of string and a heavy object such as a stone – mark the whole depth of each stripe in pencil. Continue marking lines 23cm (9in) apart across the whole wall.

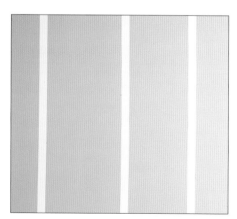

3 You are going to paint alternate stripes blue, so mask the outside edges of what will be each blue stripe with low-tack masking tape. The strips of tape should lie outside each blue stripe and inside each lilac stripe.

4 Using a 10cm (4in) brush, apply blue paint between the strips of masking tape. Make sure you work right up to the tape and allow paint to go over the tape.

5 As you work down the stripe, turn the brush sideways to make sure the paint is thoroughly worked up to the edge of the tape. Keep the brush fairly dry and not overloaded with paint. Apply two coats.

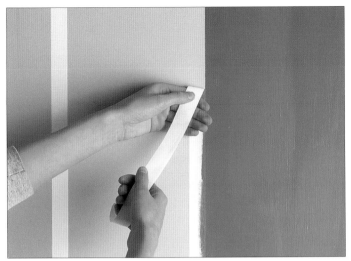

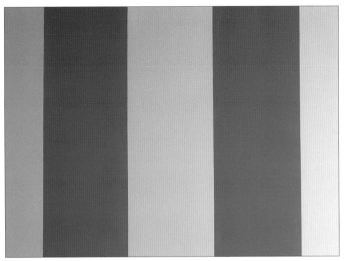

6 When the stripe is complete, gently peel off the tape to check that the paint hasn't bled underneath it. Pull gently and carefully, keeping your hands close to the wall. Continue painting the remaining stripes in the same way.

Finished effect

With these carefully chosen colours, the completed wall is bold, yet harmonious. Stripes can be painted in closely related shades for a more subtle striped effect.

Wide paint-effect stripes

Wide stripes can be made more interesting by adding ragged or sponged glaze. First paint and treat the wall with whatever paint effect you choose first. Then add the stripes in the same way as before and rag or sponge them as desired.

Pale terracotta acrylic glaze

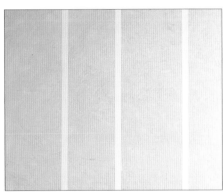

1 First prepare the wall and paint with white vinyl silk/satin latex (see p. 72). Apply the glaze and rag (see Steps 1–4 on p. 86).

2 When the whole wall is ragged, measure and mark the positions of the stripes (see p. 76). Mark the stripes with masking tape, placing the tape on the outside edges of what will be each darker stripe.

3 Apply another coat of glaze on the stripe area, making sure you fill it completely. Allow the paint to go over the tape. Rag with a piece of mutton cloth as before. When the stripe is complete, remove the tape and move on to the next stripe.

Finished effect

Ragging adds a subtle texture to these wide stripes and lifts them into something out of the ordinary.

Foam roller stripes

Create these attractive ribbon-like stripes with a specially prepared foam roller. Simply cut away sections of the foam roller to make three raised bands to which the paint adheres. As the roller is taken down the wall, the bands apply stripes of colour. Use matt emulsion/latex, thinned with water to a creamy consistency so that it soaks into the foam more easily. The coverage is not meant to be even, but the stripes can be made more or less dense, depending on the amount of pressure you use when you apply the roller. As well as a roller and paint trays, you will need a ruler and craft knife.

Dark green matt emulsion/latex, thinned with water

Medium green matt emulsion/latex, thinned with water

Light green matt emulsion/latex, thinned with water

Preparing the rollers

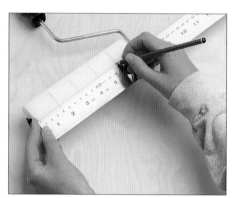

1 Take a clean foam roller and divide it into five equal sections – three bands and a space between each band. Mark the sections in pencil on the foam, taking the lines right round the roller.

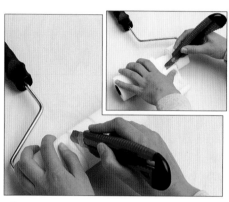

2 Using a craft knife, cut round the first and second marks. Take the knife about 12mm (½ in) into the foam. Cut across between the lines and shave the foam away, while peeling it back with the other hand (see inset).

3 Cut round the remaining pencil marks and shave away the foam at the other side of the central band, as in Step 2. The finished roller should have three raised sections to create the stripes. Cut a roller for each colour.

Measuring the wall

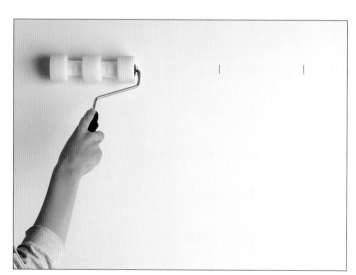

1 Divide the wall into sections the width of the foam roller and mark with pencil (see pp. 76–77 for more information on measuring up a wall for a design and dealing with obstacles).

2 At the centre of the wall, or at intervals of three or four sections, place a vertical strip of low-tack masking tape as a guide to help you keep the roller straight as you work.

Applying the stripes

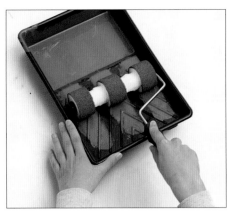

1 Dip a roller into the darkest colour. Roll it back and forth a few times on the tray to make sure that each of the raised bands is covered with paint.

2 Test the roller on some lining paper to check that it is not overloaded. You can always go over the stripes again if necessary, but it is harder to take paint away.

3 The effect varies according to the pressure you put on the roller. A light touch creates a soft look (above left). More pressure gives a denser stripe (above right).

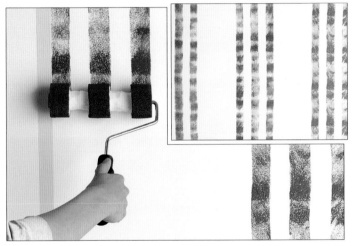

4 Starting at the right-hand corner, take the roller down the wall from top to bottom. Positioning the roller according to your marks, continue making alternate widths of stripes in dark green (see inset). Remove the strips of masking tape as you pass them.

5 Load a clean roller with the medium green and test as in Steps 1 and 2. Position the roller in between the first two widths of dark stripes and paint a section of medium green stripes.

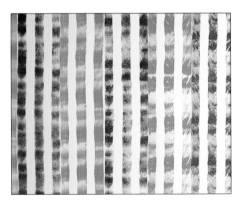

6 Continue filling the areas between the sets of dark green stripes with sets of medium green stripes.

7 Load a clean roller with the third colour and test as in Steps 1 and 2. Position the roller so that two foam bands cover the white spaces between stripes and the third paints over the stripe beneath.

8 Continue working in this way until all the white areas are covered by the third colour. If, when you have finished, any areas look too light, go over them again with the medium or light green.

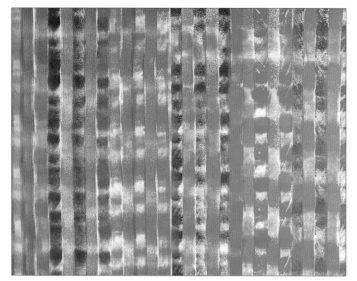

Finished effect

The completed wall is covered with stripes in the three shades of green. Some stripes are made up of two layers of different greens; others of only one layer. The irregularity of the coverage is part of the attraction. You can achieve a more subtle look by using very closely related colours, or only one or two colours on a light ground.

SUBTLE STRIPES

For this quieter treatment, the wall was first painted with cream matt emulsion/latex (see p. 72). A row of foam-roller stripes was added in one shade of pale ochre, creating a look that is calm and soothing.

Tartan

To create a simplified version of a traditional tartan, first prepare the wall with a base coat of yellow matt emulsion/latex (see p. 72). Make the sets of three stripes with a foam roller, as on pp. 90–91. You will need a foam roller and paint trays as before and a small brush for adding the single red stripes.

Yellow matt
emulsion/latex

Red matt
emulsion/latex

Light green matt
emulsion/latex

Dark green matt
emulsion/latex

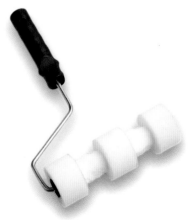

1 Cut two foam rollers – one for each shade of green – to make three raised bands with spaces between them as described in Steps 1–3 on p. 90.

2 Start at the right-hand side, one roller's width in from the corner. Dip the roller in the dark green as in Step 1 on p. 91. Start working down the wall from top to bottom.

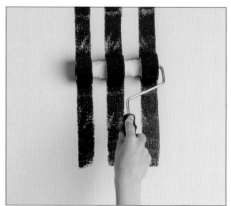

3 For this technique the stripes need to be clear and strong. As you take the roller down the wall, you may need to go back over stripes to achieve sufficient density.

4 Position the next set of stripes two rollers' width away from the first and repeat Steps 2 and 3. Continue making sets of dark stripes until you have completed the wall or room.

5 Using the second roller and lighter green paint, make the horizontal stripes. Start one roller's width away from the top of the wall and work across, going back over the stripes as before. Continue down the wall, making each set of stripes two rollers' width below the last (see inset).

6 Working down the wall, mark the centre point of each square. Make another pencil mark 12mm (½ in) to each side of the centre point of each square.

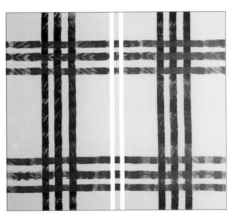

7 Place two strips of masking tape through a vertical line of squares, so that the inside edge of each is 12mm (½ in) from the centre, making a 2.5 cm (1 in) stripe between them.

8 Using a 2.5 cm (1 in) brush, stipple in the red paint between the two lengths of tape with a punching action. Use a dry brush so that paint does not seep under the tape.

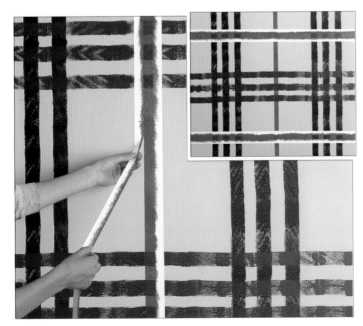

9 When the stripe is complete, remove the tape carefully. Repeat down the centre of the other squares. Repeat the process to make horizontal red stripes, this time placing lengths of tape 12mm (½ in) above and below the mark at the centre of the square (see inset).

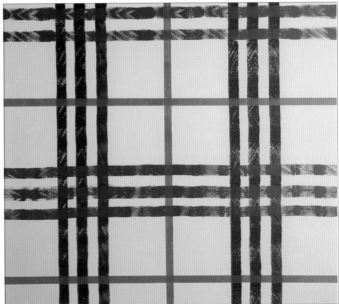

Finished effect

When complete, this vibrant tartan design makes an arresting finish for a wall. The colours can be varied to suit your own taste and decor, but it is best to echo an authentic tartan.

Stencilling

ONE OF THE OLDEST OF ALL DECORATIVE painting techniques, stencilling is also one of the easiest to master and a perfect way of creating something wholly original and unique in your home.

In stencilling, paint is applied to the wall through holes in a cut-out design on card. The design may be just a simple border or can cover a whole room. For best results,

stencilling must be neatly done. Use a 2.5cm (1in) brush or a small stencilling brush and stipple the paint on with a firm, punching action. Keep the brush dry and do not overload it or the paint will seep beneath the stencil leaving a blurred edge. Arrange your designs carefully and remember that stencils are versatile – they can be reversed, turned upside down or angled however you choose.

Three-dimensional stencilling

Stencils do not always have to be blocks of solid colour. Some variation in the depth of colour helps designs, such as leaves, look more natural and interesting and gives them a three-dimensional, textured look.

Basic stencilling

Whether the design is simple or complex, the stencilling method is much the same. You draw or trace a design, transfer it to card, and cut out the stencil. You then apply the design to the wall with paint.

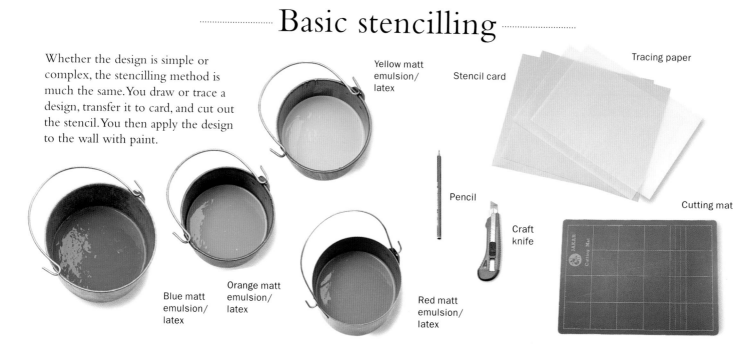

Yellow matt emulsion/ latex

Stencil card

Tracing paper

Pencil

Craft knife

Cutting mat

Blue matt emulsion/ latex

Orange matt emulsion/ latex

Red matt emulsion/ latex

Making the stencil

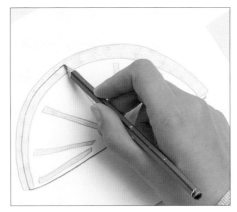

1 Put tracing paper over the orange slice drawing and trace to make the basic shape stencil. Trace along the bottom edge, but work just in from the outside, curved edge.

2 Put a fresh piece of tracing paper over the orange slice drawing and trace the detail, or shaded areas.

Draw or trace the pictures you want to use as stencils. For a simple stencil such as the lemon, simply trace the shape. For a more complex stencil, such as the orange, you will need to make two stencils, one for the shape and one for the details.

3 Trace the lemon shape as a simple outline. You now have three traces – one for the lemon and two for the orange slice.

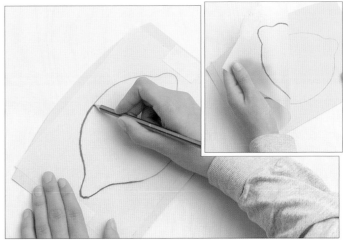

4 Place a tracing face down over a piece of stencil card. Go over the lines, pressing as hard as you can so that the line transfers to the card below. Take away the tracing paper to reveal the image on the card below (see inset).

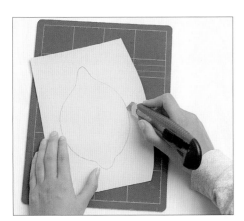

5 Place one of the stencil cards on a cutting mat. Using a craft knife, carefully cut round the pencil line to leave the stencil shape. Repeat to cut the other two stencils.

Orange shape stencil

Lemon stencil

Orange detail stencil

6 You now have three stencils on stencil card: the lemon, the basic orange slice shape and the detail of the orange slice.

Stencilling onto the wall

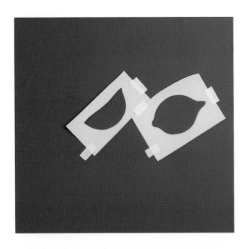

1 Prepare the wall with a coat of matt emulsion/latex (see p. 72). Having worked out your design, tape both outline stencils to the wall. When using more than one stencil as here, position both, stencil, then position both again.

2 Apply colour to the lemon stencil. Use a dry brush and hold down the edge of the stencil so the paint does not bleed under it. Work with a stippling action to fill the shape and pay special attention to the edges. Paint the orange in the same way (see inset).

3 Remove the stencils then re-position for the next pair. Place them carefully, making sure that they sit on the same base line.

4 Repeat Step 2 and continue stencilling until you have a line of as many oranges and lemons as you want.

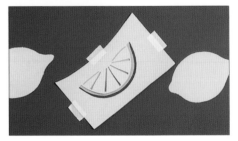

5 Take the orange detail stencil and position it very carefully so that it fits neatly over the basic orange shape stencil.

6 Add the darker orange-red with a pouncing, stippling action as before, making sure that all areas of the stencil are filled in.

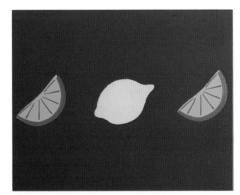

7 Complete the rest of the orange slices in the same way. If desired, you can add extra detail by hand such as a touch of green at the end of the lemon.

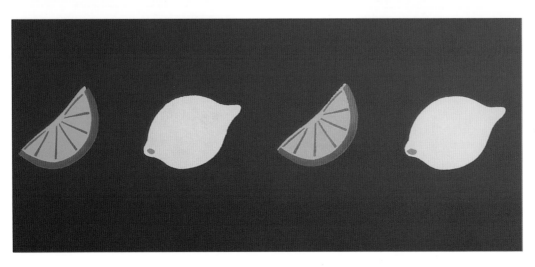

Finished effect

A simple block stencil design makes an effective border at dado level or could be used round a door or kitchen cupboards. Plan your stencil design carefully before you start and don't overdo it. Simplicity is the key to successful stencilling.

Stencilling an all-over design

You can stencil a whole wall in just the same way as the border stencil, but you do have to take care with the arrangement of the stencil on the wall. Check the fit first to help you decide on the spacing between the stencils. Start with a complete design just below the ceiling or cornice.

Pale green matt emulsion/latex

Grey-blue matt emulsion/latex

1 Apply the first vertical line of stencils. Keep the same distance between each stencil – here, 4cm (1½ in) between the bottom of one and the top of the next. For the next row, place the stencils so that each one nestles between the adjacent two in the first row.

2 For the third row, align each stencil with those in the first row. The fourth row should again be staggered to align with the second row. Continue in this way, alternating rows to create the overall pattern.

Finished effect

Although this is quite a complex stencil, the overall effect is restful and pleasing. The colours tone well together so that the effect is subtle rather than striking.

Three-dimensional stencilling

Sometimes it is helpful to vary the intensity of the colour on the stencil to achieve a more textured, three-dimensional result. To do this, apply the colour by stippling strongly at the outside edges and more lightly in the centre of the image.

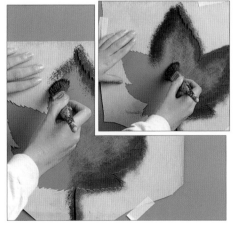

1 Fix the stencil to the wall in the usual way. Stipple strongly around the outside of the stencil, applying several layers and leave the centre clearer. Then stipple the centre with a lighter touch (see inset).

Finished technique

The completed leaf stippled in this way has a more lively, interesting effect than a block stencil. This technique is particularly suited to natural subjects such as leaves and flowers.

Faux Finishes

THE AIM OF A FAUX FINISH is to simulate the effect of a natural material, such as marble or wood, in paint. Properly done, this can add a touch of luxury to a room. Before attempting to do any of these faux finishes, always look at the real thing or, failing that, good

photographs. Your painted version doesn't have to be an exact copy, but it should have the character of the original. Be inventive with colour. Stone, such as marble and porphyry, comes in a range of shades and you can add your own tones. Tortoiseshell looks good in blues and greens as well as natural colours.

Woodgraining is an exacting craft and takes some skill to do. Techniques vary according to the type of wood you want to imitate. Again, look at a sample of the wood first and study its grain, colour and growth patterns. The example described here is for mahogany, but other woods, such as pine, oak, and walnut, can also be painted.

Trompe l'oeil means to deceive the eye and it imitates not a substance but actual objects. Shading is added to give the object a three-dimensional quality. The simplest form of trompe l'oeil is to paint the wall to look like real recessed panels, with clever shading. Alternatively, try painting objects – a vase on the wall above a shelf, an umbrella stand in a hallway – or a whole fake window with a scene beyond. Another form of trompe l'oeil is to juxtapose objects painted in light and dark shades of the same colour so that they stand out from each other.

Marbled blocks
Marbling has been applied to this wall in oblongs to make it look as though it is constructed of large marble blocks. Fine lines have been painted around the blocks to imitate grouting.

Marbling

Marbling can be applied on walls or on smaller areas such as fireplaces. Here we show a simplified version. You apply different colours of glaze (see p. 70) and merge them, first by ragging, then with a feather, and lastly with a soft brush. You need a badger brush (see p. 66).

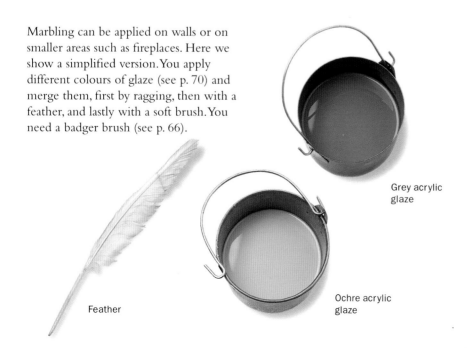

Feather

Grey acrylic glaze

Ochre acrylic glaze

1 Prepare the wall and paint with white vinyl silk/satin latex (see p. 72). If you are marbling in blocks, measure and mark the wall (see p. 78). The blocks shown here are 30 x 51cm (12 x 20in). Apply the two acrylic glazes in a random diagonal arrangement.

2 Rag the glazes so that they blend together (see p. 86 for more information on ragging). Make sure that there is a reasonable balance between the two colours.

3 Dunk the feather in water. Dab the ragged glaze with the side of the feather to create the veins of the marble. Work diagonally with slight jigging movements, making sure that the veins all go in roughly the same direction.

4 Take a badger brush and work lightly from side to side over the area to soften the veins and blend the two colours together.

5 Using a piece of mutton cloth over your thumb, wipe away any uneven edges. Work fast before the paint dries.

6 Repeat Steps 1–5 until all the blocks on the wall are glazed, ragged, and marked as described.

7 When the wall is complete, mix a slightly darker version of the grey glaze. Using an artist's brush, carefully draw round the edges of all the squares to suggest grouting lines.

Finished effect

If marbling in blocks like this, don't feel you have to make each block look exactly the same. They should be reasonably uniform, but some should be slightly stronger in colour than others to look convincing.

Porphyry flick

This subtle effect, also known as flyspecking, re-creates the look of granular porphyry rock. The surface is prepared with vinyl silk/satin latex and glaze (see p. 70). You then flick darker, more concentrated glaze, mixed with less water than usual, over the wall with a 2.5cm (1in) brush.

Parchment-coloured acrylic glaze

Concentrated glaze with raw umber and burnt umber pigments

1 Prepare the wall and paint with white vinyl silk/satin latex (see p. 72). Apply parchment-coloured glaze and sponge lightly (see p. 87) to achieve a subtle effect.

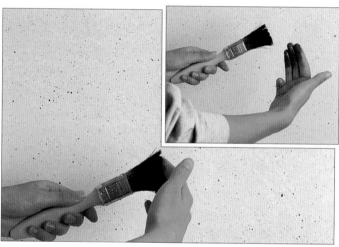

2 Dip a 2.5cm (1in) brush into the concentrated glaze. Holding the brush in your left hand, stroke the end quite firmly with your right hand so that the paint flicks onto the wall. One dip should enable you to flick for about five minutes. Your fingers will get covered with paint (see inset) so wipe them with a rag occasionally.

Final effect

For this effect to look its best, the dots of darker glaze should be varied in size. This happens naturally – the dots are largest when you start flicking a new brushful of paint and gradually become smaller as you work. When flicking, cover everything else in the room to protect it.

Woodgraining

Woodgraining transforms a cheap door into one of glowing mahogany. Here we show a simplified version. You paint and apply glaze (see p. 70) to the door and than make the grain markings. You will need a mottler and flogging brush (see p. 66).

Rich brown glaze mixed from Vandyke brown and burnt sienna

Cinnamon quick-drying/acrylic latex eggshell

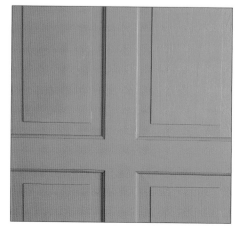

1 First paint the door with cinnamon quick-drying/acrylic latex eggshell. Follow the usual order for painting doors (see p. 75).

2 Once the egg-shell is dry, apply brown acrylic glaze to one of the panels of the door with a 2.5cm (1in) brush.

3 Take a mottler (see p. 66) and hold it firmly between your thumb and your first two fingers (see inset). Using gentle swooping movements, move the brush up each panel to produce a tapering elliptical grain. Then repeat Steps 2–3 on the other panels.

4 Take a badger brush and brush very gently from side to side over each panel to soften the markings made by the mottler.

5 Using a flogging brush, apply a coat of glaze to the stiles. Hold the base of the bristles against the door and use some pressure to get a coarse drag.

6 Drag each stile and the mouldings in the same way, working across the horizontal stiles and down the vertical stiles.

7 Apply a second coat of glaze to a panel. Using the flogging brush, flog up the panel lightly – using gentle beating movements in an upward direction with a firm consistent action. Repeat on the remaining panels and on the stiles. Flog up the vertical stiles and across the horizontal stiles.

Finished effect

Adding a second layer of glaze to the door strengthens the wood effect and the flogging action adds depth and texture. This technique creates a mahogany effect, but you can vary the technique to imitate other woods such as oak and pine.

Tortoiseshell

This effect imitates the look of real tortoiseshell and can be used to create panels or on smaller areas such as dadoes. On a glowing orange base, you apply and rag a brown glaze (see p. 70). You then add daubs of a more concentrated glaze mixture and soften these with a dry brush. You need a badger brush and a small 2.5cm (1in) brush (see p. 66).

Orange vinyl silk/satin latex

Brown acrylic glaze

Concentrated brown glaze

1 Prepare the area that is to be tortoise-shelled and paint in rich orange vinyl silk/satin latex (see p. 72).

2 Unless the area is very small you will have to apply glaze and rag in sections (see p. 74). Lay the brown glaze over the area. Work in a diagonal direction and don't worry about making the coverage too even. Rag over the glaze (see p. 86).

3 Dip a 2.5cm (1in) brush into the darker, more concentrated glaze. Daub the area with clusters of colour. Keep the daubs random – they should not be placed in a regular pattern.

4 Gently brush all over the area with a badger brush to soften and blend the daubs of colour and create the tortoiseshell look. Apply another coat of glaze and repeat Steps 2–4. When the paint is thoroughly dry, finish with a coat of gloss acrylic varnish (see p. 73).

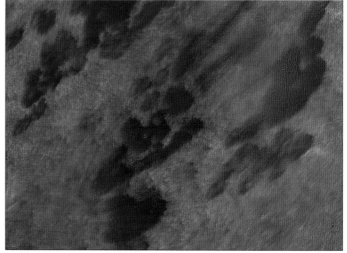

Final effect

Applying two layers of glaze gives the tortoiseshell greater depth and effect. It does not have to be done in colours that a real tortoise would wear – greens and blues can also look splendid.

Malachite

Like tortoiseshell, malachite imitates a natural substance –
a beautiful greeny-blue mineral. You prepare the wall with
green vinyl silk/satin latex and add a blue-black glaze. You
then work over the glaze with a small piece of card, scraping
the malachite pattern and revealing some of the green base.

Small piece
of light card

Green vinyl silk/
satin latex

Blue-black
acrylic glaze

1 Prepare the wall and paint with green vinyl silk/satin latex (see p. 72). Then lay the blue-black glaze roughly over the same area (see inset). Don't worry if it looks uneven.

2 Take a small piece of light card, about the size of a business card. Hold it flat between your thumb and three fingers as shown above.

3 Pressing the card against the wall, work round in circles, scraping a pattern in the paint. Stop every now and then and wipe excess paint off the card onto a rag.

4 Work first one way and then the other until a circle is complete. Fill in little bits with the end of the card. Circles can be different sizes but keep them close together.

Finished effect

Malachite makes a wonderful
jewel-like finish for a dado border
or other small area in a room.
The patterns shouldn't be too regular – look at some real malachite
for inspiration before you start.
Finish the effect with a coat of
satin acrylic varnish (see p. 73)
for an authentic sheen.

Trompe l'oeil

Trompe l'oeil gives a flat painted object a three-dimensional look with shadow lines. You could paint a panel like this to fill an area above a door or panel a whole wall under a dado. You will need a dragging brush and a glider (see pp. 66-67).

Terracotta acrylic glaze

Pale grey matt emulsion/ latex

Dark grey-blue matt emulsion/ latex

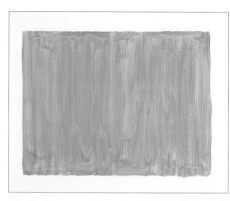

1 First prepare the wall with white vinyl silk/ satin latex (see p. 72). Measure and mark the panels on the wall (see p. 79). Apply acrylic glaze to the centre section of the panel.

2 Take a dragging brush and drag the panel firmly (see p. 84). The dragging should have a pronounced effect.

3 Wipe off any paint running over the marks for the central section of the panel with a damp cloth wrapped around your thumb.

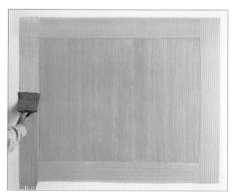

4 Apply glaze to the stiles marked around the panel. Drag with a gliding brush for a more subtle effect. Work across horizontal panels and down vertical panels.

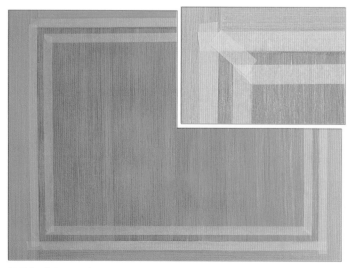

5 Apply low-tack tape all around the outside of the central panel. Apply more tape 2cm (¾in) in from that, as shown above. At the top left, mark a line from corner to corner between the tapes and place a piece of tape above that line (see inset). Tape the bottom right corner in the same way.

6 Apply light grey matt emulsion/latex to the area between the tapes to the left of the panel and at the bottom. Stipple the paint on with a dry brush so that the paint does not bleed under the tape. Wipe the brush on cloth or newspaper from time to time to keep it dry.

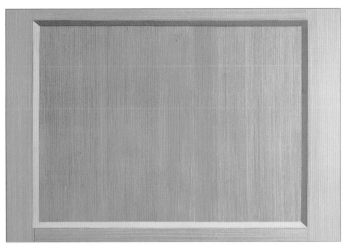

7 Move the tape at the top left corner so that it lies below the line from corner to corner. Adjust the tape at the bottom right corner in the same way. Apply dark grey matt emulsion/latex to the top and right, stippling it on with a 2.5cm (1in) brush as before.

8 Remove the tapes and your panel should look like the example above – a central dragged panel surrounded by dragged stiles. There should be narrow light grey lines to the left and along the bottom and dark grey lines across the top and to the right.

9 Apply a length of tape just outside the pale grey lines to the left and along the bottom of the panel. Apply more tape about 6mm (¼in) in from that. Mitre the corners as before. Stipple between these tapes in dark grey, again using a very dry brush so the paint does not bleed.

10 Tape across the top and to the right of the panel, just inside the dark grey, and again 6mm (¼ in) in from that. Mitre corners as before and stipple in light grey.

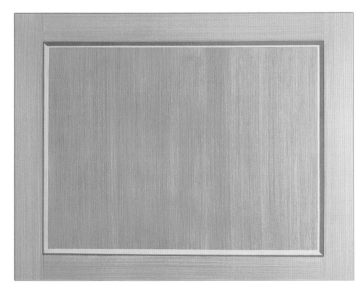

Finished effect

When the panel is complete, the lines of dark and light grey will create a three-dimensional effect as through the light is falling on a recessed panel from the right. If making more than one panel, remember that the left stile of one makes the right stile of the next and so on.

VARIATION

If you want to paint objects such as this umbrella as trompe l'oeil, complete the object first and then add shadow lines in dark and light grey as described to give the three-dimensional look. Always check the way the natural light falls on the area you are painting. This will dictate the positioning of your shadow lines.

Antique Finishes

THE AIM OF ANTIQUE FINISHES is to give a naturally aged look to a wall or other surface. Before trying one of these techniques, think of old buildings you have seen when travelling or in photographs. Bear their faded colours and uneven surfaces in mind when mixing your glaze. Aged effects look their best in subtle, gentle shades, not glowing primaries.

Although they are extremely effective, antique finishes are the simplest of all paint techniques for the complete beginner to try. Irregularity is part of the charm of finishes such as frottage, distressing, and rough plaster so it does not matter if you go slightly wrong. Frottage is the easiest of all, but ironically appears complex and interesting. You apply glaze in the normal way, then lift it off with newspaper.

Distressing and rough plaster

Distressing is particularly suitable for woodwork, such as doors, cupboards, and skirting/baseboards and can also be used on furniture, picture frames, and other wooden items. You apply the glaze and then sweep over it with steel wool, lifting some of the glaze to create a slightly worn, battered look. Again, slightly uneven results are part of the attraction of the technique. Rough plaster, with its deliberate ridges and texture, gives a relaxed, rustic feel and is ideal for uneven surfaces.

These finishes are not suited to sophisticated, highly formal rooms, but all can look extremely attractive in the right surroundings, evoking the style of a fading Italian villa or a crumbling country cottage.

Subtle ageing

This warm yellow is a perfect shade for frottage, giving a look that is interesting but not overwhelming. The uneven covering of paint adds a visual texture to the wall.

Frottage

For this antique effect, you apply glaze (see p. 70) over the base colour an area at a time. While the glaze is still wet you apply a sheet of newspaper on top of it and pat all over gently. The paper removes glaze unevenly to create a random organic pattern.

Newspaper

Blue–green
acrylic glaze

1 Prepare the wall and paint with white vinyl silk/satin latex (see p. 72). Apply the glaze to an area roughly 90cm (36in) square in the top right corner of the wall (see p. 74). Use rough criss-crossing strokes (see p. 82).

2 Take a double sheet of newspaper and place it over the glazed area. Pat firmly over the newspaper for a moment or two so it soaks up some of the glaze from the wall.

3 Peel the newspaper off the wall and repeat the process over the rest of the glazed area with clean sheets of newspaper. Make sure every bit of glaze is frottaged, overlapping if necessary. It does not matter how irregular the effect appears.

4 Apply glaze to the next section of wall and repeat Steps 2 and 3 to frottage. Repeat until the whole wall is finished.

5 Once the wall is finished, stand back and look at the overall effect. If any areas do not look right, go over them again with fresh sheets of newspaper.

Finished effect

Frottaging gives a subtly aged look to a wall. Part of the charm of this effect is its unpredictability – it never looks quite the same twice. The finished look depends on the consistency of the paint, the absorbency of the paper, and the pressure that you apply.

Distressing

Distressing creates an attractively aged effect and looks good on doors. Paint the door with quick-drying/acrylic latex eggshell and then apply a coat of glaze (see p. 70). Go over the glaze with a handful of steel wool. If you are distressing a large area, wear gloves as the steel wool can irritate your skin.

Steel wool

Blue-grey quick-drying/
acrylic latex eggshell

Dark blue
acrylic glaze

1 Prepare the door and paint with a coat of quick-drying/acrylic latex eggshell, following the order for painting a door (see p. 75). Apply a coat of dark blue acrylic glaze to the first panel (see inset).

2 Take a handful of steel wool and sweep up and down the glazed panel, lifting some of the glaze. The abrasive steel wool leaves a texture on the glaze as you work.

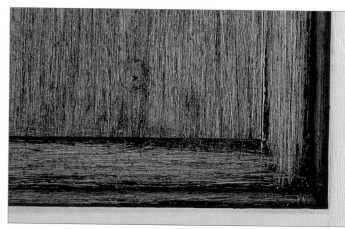

3 Allow glaze to collect in the corners of a panel and remove more at the centre, which would naturally become more worn. Continue glazing and distressing the door, working across horizontal stiles and up and down vertical stiles and panels.

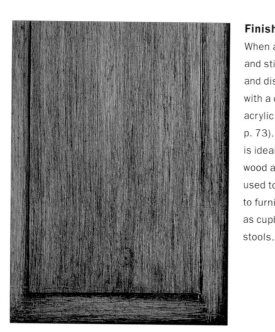

Finished effect
When all the panels and stiles are glazed and distressed, finish with a coat of flat acrylic varnish (see p. 73). This technique is ideal for treating wood and can also be used to add interest to furniture, such as cupboards and stools.

VARIATION

Skirting/baseboards can be distressed. For a subtle look (top), lay the glaze thinly and immediately go over it gently with steel wool. For a more pronounced effect (bottom), lay the glaze thickly and leave for for a few minutes before distressing vigorously.

Rough plaster

Rough plaster is a good finish for an uneven wall. First seal the wall with a coat of PVA bond and leave it to dry. To make a plasterer's hawk for holding plaster, take a piece of board about 30cm (12in) square and screw a length of dowel into the base.

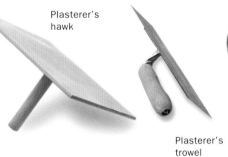
Plasterer's hawk

Plasterer's trowel

Orange matt emulsion/latex

1 Take a bucket of water. Add finishing (not undercoat) plaster, stirring all the time with a stick. See maker's instructions for quantities, but the mixture should be thick enough to sit on your hawk without dripping.

2 Load some plaster onto the hawk with a flat plasterer's trowel. Mix the plaster for a moment or two by lifting it and turning it with the trowel to improve the texture.

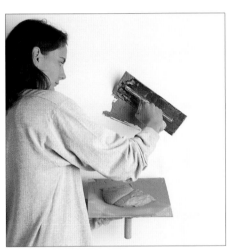

3 Holding the hawk near the wall, load the trowel with plaster. Spread it onto the wall with upward strokes.

4 Continue spreading plaster onto the wall. Ridges will form where the trowel stops and starts, but these give texture to the finish. Keep the ridges reasonably uniform – too many can look messy.

5 Check that you are happy with the look. Smooth away any excess ridges before leaving the plaster to dry overnight. The next day, apply a coat of white, watered-down matt emulsion/latex (80 per cent paint and 20 per cent water). This soaks into the plaster and evens out the texture.

Finished effect

Once the watered-down emulsion/latex is dry, paint the plaster with two coats of matt emulsion/latex or colourwash it (see pp. 82–83) for an even more interesting effect. This rough finish would suit a garden room or conservatory.

Tiling

TILES ARE DECORATIVE AND PRACTICAL, the most hard-wearing of all wallcoverings. They withstand quantities of water and steam in the bathroom, and are easy to wipe clean of grease and dirt in the kitchen.

Tiles are available in a wide range of plain colours and patterns. Simple white tiles are always effective, but ornate designs give a room a more flamboyant feel. Try mixing different kinds – combinations of white and coloured tiles, or alternate plain and patterned, for example. Most tiles are square, but rectangular tiles, useful for making borders or edging, are also available, as well as tiny mosaic tiles of only 2cm (¾in) square.

Tiling is not difficult but you need to prepare the wall carefully and make sure it is clean and smooth before you start or the tiles will not sit neatly. If you want the tiled area to be completely waterproof, use waterproof tile adhesive and grouting.

Tiles can be used purely decoratively to make a frame round a doorway or alcove. Particularly special tiles could be just arranged on the wall like pictures.

Tiled simplicity
The simplest possible look for a bathroom, pure white tiles always look fresh and appealing. They are the most practical and long-lasting of surfaces if properly applied.

Tiling a wall

For successful tiling, start by fixing a wooden batten as a straight horizontal base for your tiles to sit on. Check that it is straight with a spirit level. You then spread tile adhesive on the wall and apply the tiles row by row, using plastic tile spacers in between each tile. Once all the tiles are in place, you apply grouting paste to fill the spaces between the tiles. Finally wipe the tiles clean and polish them with a dry cloth.

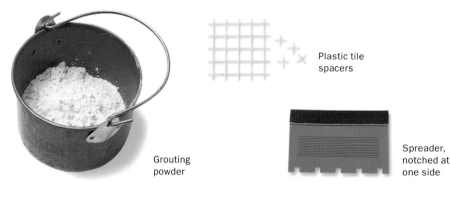

Plastic tile spacers

Grouting powder

Spreader, notched at one side

CUTTING TILES

Inevitably you will have to cut some tiles to fit awkward spaces. If you are tiling a small area and have only a few tiles to cut to size, a small, simple tile cutter as shown here should be adequate. If you have a large amount to deal with, it might be worth investing in a more efficient tool to make your task easier. There is a range of different types to choose from.

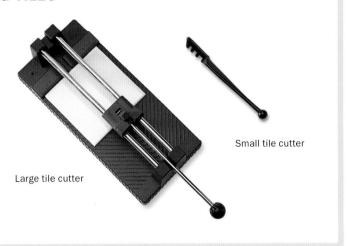

Small tile cutter

Large tile cutter

Finding a level horizontal

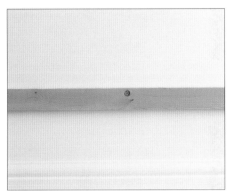

1 Take one of the tiles you are going to use. Place it on top of the skirting/baseboard and move it across the wall, marking at the top of the tile with pencil to find the highest point – most skirting/baseboards are not quite level.

2 Check the highest point with a spirit level. This is the height of one row of tiles. Add 4mm to allow for two grouting lines and draw a line right across the wall at this level (see inset).

3 Take a length of 5 x 2.5cm (2 x 1in) wood and nail it to the wall. The top should be on the pencil line drawn across the wall 4mm above the highest point marked. The wood makes a horizontal base for the tiles.

Fixing tiles

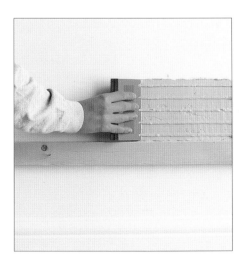

1 Using the notched side of the spreader, spread tile adhesive right across the wall to the height of one row of tiles. Spread evenly and keep a constant pressure to produce ridges in the adhesive. These ridges create suction and help hold the tiles to the wall.

2 Start applying tiles to the wall in a corner. The tiles should rest on the batten.

3 As you work, place plastic spacers between each tile. These keep the tiles the correct distant apart and will be grouted over later.

4 Apply another band of adhesive as in Step 1 and apply the next row of tiles. Keep cleaning the faces of the tiles as you work to re-move any adhesive before it sets.

5 Continue tiling until the whole wall above the batten is completed. Remove the batten from the wall.

6 Spread adhesive on the area above the skirting/baseboard and apply the bottom row of tiles. Most skirting/baseboards are not quite straight, so fill any extra space below the tiles with pieces of card.

7 In order to fit the depth or width of the space to be tiled, it may be necessary to cut tiles. There are several tools for doing this (see p. 111).

Grouting tiles

1 Mix the grouting powder with water to a thick, creamy consistency. Using the flat side of your spreader, put some grout onto the tiled wall and spread it across diagonally with sweeping strokes, allowing it to sink into the spaces between the tiles.

2 Continue spread-ing until all the joints are well filled – don't try to force grout into the joints. Wipe as much of the excess grouting as you can off the tile surfaces with the spreader.

3 Wipe the tiles and grouting over with a wet sponge. Push the grout into joins with the sponge to even up the lines as much as possible. Take out any pieces of card under the bottom row and fill the spaces with grouting. Allow the grout to dry and then wipe over with a dry cloth to remove the powdery deposit and polish the tiles (see inset).

Finished effect

The tiling on the completed wall should look neat and regular with even lines of grouting separating the tiles. Note that if you are tiling a wall behind a bath or shower it is best to use waterproof adhesive.

VARIATIONS

Tiled border

Tiling can be decorative as well as practical. Here, two different sorts of tiles are used to make an attractive border on an alcove. The square tiles are fixed all round the alcove, with a hexagonal tile at each corner.

Decorative tiles

These tiles have been used just as decorative accents on a plain white wall. This would be an ideal way to display some really special tiles that might be too expensive to use over a whole wall.

Wallpapering

WALLPAPER IS A HARD-WEARING and decorative wallcovering and a huge range of papers in different colours, patterns, and textures is now available. In fact, choosing what paper to buy can be the hardest part of wallpapering. Before you select your paper, make sure you have estimated the amount you need correctly, allowing for any wastage for pattern matching. Although you may be able to buy an extra roll if you need, the colours in different batches of paper can vary slightly. Wallpaper is generally thought of as most suitable for sitting rooms, dining rooms, and bedrooms, but it can be used successfully in kitchens and even bathrooms. Special papers with a sheen are available for use in these rooms, but a few coats of flat acrylic varnish (see p. 73) on an ordinary paper makes the surface just as practical and easy to wipe clean.

Preparation

If your room has lots of irregular corners and sloping ceilings, think twice about using wallpaper. And if this is your first attempt at wallpapering, choose a fairly simple pattern that won't be too problematic to match across widths. Always prepare the wall carefully first and strip off any old paper completely. Get everything ready and provide yourself with a long table on which to cut and paste the paper. These are available from hire shops. Work slowly and systematically – a rushed wallpapering job will always look just that. A key task is to establish the vertical on the wall. If your first width is crooked, all the subsequent ones will be too. Check with your paper supplier on the right sort of paste for your paper. There is a range of ready-mixed adhesives and adhesives you mix yourself.

Varnished wallpaper
This patterned wallpaper makes a richly colourful backdrop for simple white bathroom fittings. If the wallpaper is given several coats of varnish, it can withstand splashes of water and bathroom steam.

Wallpapering

Successful wallpapering needs care and attention. First you must decide on where in the room you will start papering. Then measure the drop and cut the lengths, matching any repeat pattern carefully. Mix the paste and start hanging the paper length by length, making sure that each one is neatly trimmed and finished before going onto the next. For how to deal with special problems such as light switches, and papering round doors and corners, see pp. 118–119.

Other useful equipment for wallpapering:
Plumb line and pencil
Steel ruler
Sponge
Pasting table
Step ladder

Large scissors   Pasting brush   Seam roller   Wallpaper brush

Order of papering a room

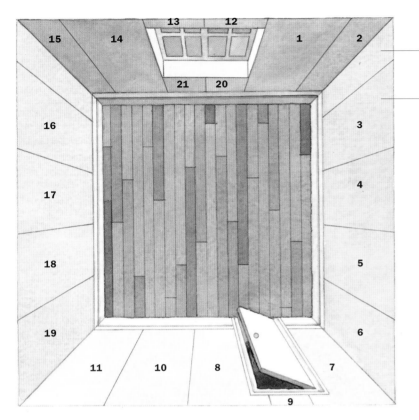

Width cut and fitted round corner

Full width

In general, you start papering next to a window and work away from the light. Joins will not then cast a shadow and will be less noticeable. But in a room with a chimney breast, centre the first length on the chimney breast and work outwards from there. The diagram shows a suitable order for wallpapering an average room.

Preparation

ESTABLISHING THE VERTICAL

It is vital to establish the vertical before you start wallpapering. Each time you start on a new wall, mark the vertical again.

To establish the vertical, hang a plumb line from the picture rail (or dado if applicable) or from the ceiling if papering the whole wall. Mark the vertical line with pencil and use this to make sure you hang the first strip straight.

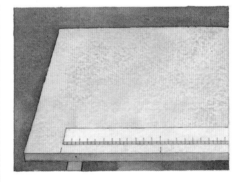

Mark your table into 30cm (12in) sections to speed measuring. If your lengths are short – for example, if you are just papering above or below a dado – you may be able to mark the whole length onto the table.

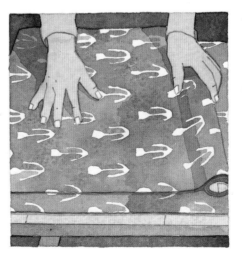

Cut each length, allowing about 5cm (2in) excess top and bottom. Use the first drop as a guide to match the pattern for subsequent drops. You will lose some paper in order to match the pattern, but some of this can form the trimming allowance. Number each sheet at the top.

Pasting

1 This is the basic method for mixing paste, but follow the manufacturer's instructions for quantities. Put some water in a bucket and stir. Add some powder to the swirling water and mix to a creamy consistency. The powder swells so don't add too much too quickly.

2 Place the first length of paper on the table, right side down. Using an ordinary 10cm (4in) brush, put some paste on the paper and brush to the outside. Continue pasting, always working from the middle to the edges until the paper is covered but not oversoaked.

Hanging paper

1 Fold the ends of the pasted length to the middle so you can drape the whole sheet over your arm without getting paste on yourself. Hold it with the marked and numbered top of the length towards you.

2 Unfold the first part and hang the sheet of wallpaper on the wall, using your vertical pencil line as a guide. Leave about 5cm (2in) at the top for trimming as allowed. Brush with a wallpaper brush to push out any air bubbles.

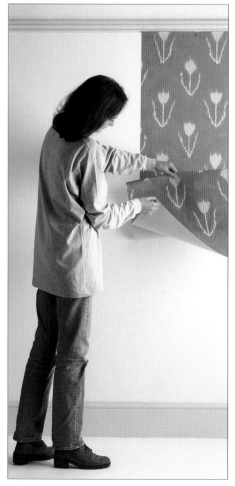

3 Open out the other fold as shown. Make sure it follows the vertical and allow any excess to overlap the skirting/baseboard at the bottom. Brush out any air bubbles as in Step 2.

4 Using the back of your scissors, push the wallpaper right into the join with the ceiling or picture rail and crease (see top). Peel the paper back and cut the excess away along the crease very carefully (see above).

5 Press the paper back onto the wall and brush again to remove any bubbles. Trim excess at the skirting/baseboard in exactly the same way as before.

6 Take the second length of paper, folded in the same way as the first. Hang it as before, butting it right up to the first sheet and matching the pattern.

7 As you work down, make sure that the pattern is still matching. Brush the sheet as in Step 2 and trim the excess as in Steps 4 and 5.

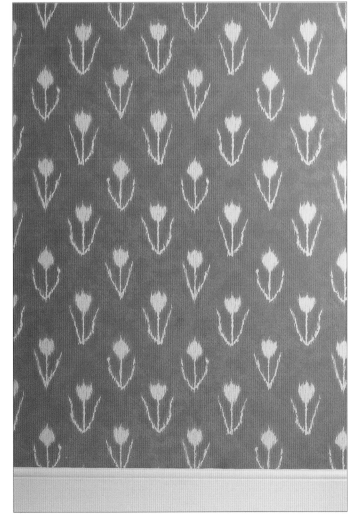

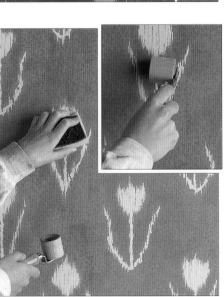

8 Take a small sponge and a seam roller. Work down the paper, wiping away any excess paste from the join with the sponge then rolling the join with the seam roller (see inset). It is important to wipe first so that you don't spread any excess glue. Continue papering until the wall is complete.

Finished effect

The completed wall with pattern matching across the lengths and excess neatly trimmed at the top and bottom.

Wallpapering difficult areas

Internal corners

Never try to paste a whole piece of wallpaper round a corner – it will looked creased and awkward. Cut the paper so that it extends to only about 12mm (½in) round the corner and then hang the remaining part of the length, allowing it to overlap slightly. If this remaining section is very narrow, don't use it and hang a new complete length instead.

On external corners, don't make the join right on the corner where it can be easily damaged. As on all corners, try and position the join as unobtrusively as possible.

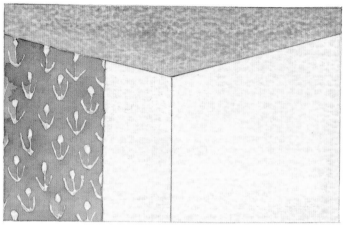

1 Before hanging the last length of paper before a corner, measure the distance between the previous drop and the corner. Check this measurement at the top and bottom of the wall and add 12mm (½in).

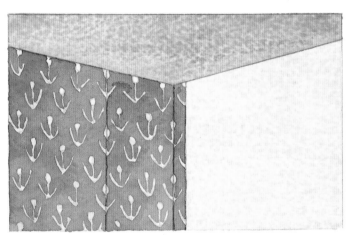

2 Cut the next length to this width and paste into place, allowing the 12mm (½in) extra to go round the corner.

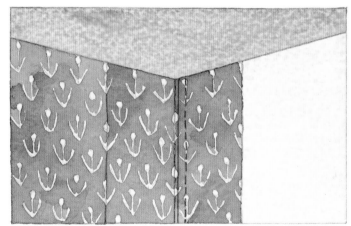

3 Place the remaining section of the paper into place on the new wall, allowing it to cover the overlap and matching it with the vertical marked on the wall.

External corners

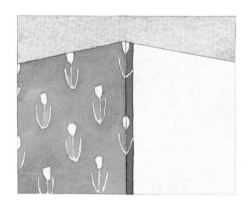

1 Measure the distance between the last length and the corner as for internal corners, but add 2.5cm (1in). Cut the next length to this measurement and hang, allowing the extra 2.5cm (1in) to fold round the corner.

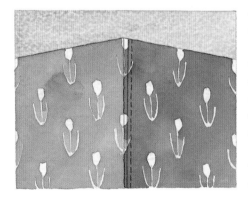

2 Hang the remaining part of the length so that it covers the overlap by about 12mm (½in). Position it against a vertical line marked on the wall as usual. Do not butt it right up to the corner – joins on corners can tear.

Wallpapering round a door

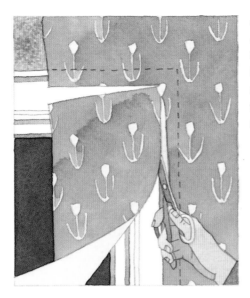

1 Hang a full length of paper allowing it to overlap the door. Cut off most of the excess hanging over the door, leaving about 2.5 cm (1in).

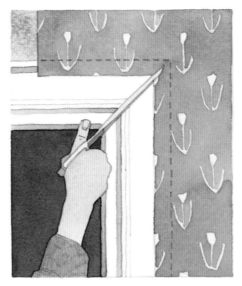

2 Make a diagonal cut into the corner so that the paper can be brushed down neatly into the join between the door frame and the wall.

3 Brush the paper into the join between the door frame and the wall then crease and trim as in Steps 4–5 on p. 117.

4 Repeat at the other side of the door and fill the space above the door with a separate length of paper.

Wallpapering round a flush light switch

1 Before wallpapering, turn off the electricity and remove the switch cover. Wallpaper over the backplate. Make two diagonal slashes in the paper over the backplate.

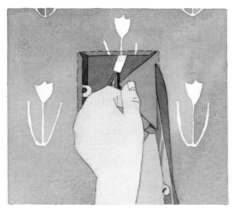

2 Insert the scissors into the slashes and cut away the paper over the backplate leaving a margin of 6mm (¼in). Snip diagonally into each corner.

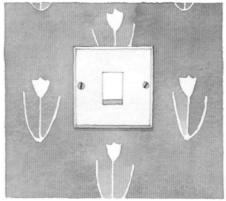

3 Replace the cover, tucking the margins of paper neatly underneath.

Fabric

FABRIC-COVERED WALLS lend a feeling of elegance and luxury to a room. They look warm and comforting and absorb sound. Fabric is best for rooms such as dining rooms or bedrooms, which do not get heavy use. It would not be suitable for children's rooms since you have no hope of wiping away any dirty fingermarks or scrawls from felt-tip pens.

The fabric is stapled to a wooden frame that has been fixed to the wall. Any fabric can be used. It does not have to be expensive, but it should be sturdy enough not to pull out of line when it is stretched and stapled to the frame. Baize and felt have the right sort of solidity, but a firm cotton is perfectly good.

An easy way to use fabric is to cover just the wall area below dado level. Add ribbon borders top and bottom to hide the staples. Alternatively, cover the whole wall, but make sure your chosen fabric is available in suitable widths. A false dado band can be added to cover joins and create extra interest. Covering walls with fabric is not difficult, but it is useful to have another pair of hands available to hold the fabric while you stretch it over the wooden frame and staple it in place.

Green baize wall

Here, the whole wall has been covered in green baize fabric. A band of ribbon has been added at dado level to hide staples and two rows of gleaming brass studs hammered along its length for decorative interest.

Making the fabric panel

To cover a wall area with fabric, first fix a wooden frame to the wall. You then staple wadding to the wooden frame to cushion the fabric and add padding and softness. Next staple the fabric to the frame in the same way and glue strips of ribbon over the fabric edges to hide the stapling.

Staple gun

Fabric glue

Wadding   Ribbon

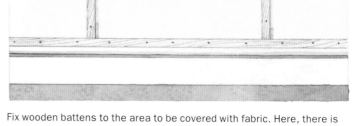

Fix wooden battens to the area to be covered with fabric. Here, there is one batten on the wall below the dado and one above the skirting/baseboard. Fix vertical battens at intervals of about 1m (39in).

1 Cut the wadding roughly to fit – any excess can be trimmed later. Begin stapling the wadding to the top horizontal batten. Pull the wadding tight after each staple before going onto the next one. When the wadding has been stapled all along the top batten, staple it to the vertical battens. A couple of staples on each one should be enough.

2 Staple across the bottom batten as before. Smooth the wadding down firmly with your hand between each staple, making sure that it lies flat against the wall.

3 Take a steel ruler and hold it against the wadding above the skirting/baseboard, Carefully cut away excess wadding with a craft knife, pulling it away as you cut.

4 Cut the fabric to fit between top and bottom battens. Staple to the top batten. Staple every 7 or 8cm (3in) or so, pulling it smooth and taut each time. It helps to have someone holding the fabric as you staple.

5 Pull the fabric at the bottom so it is taut against the wall. Staple at the centre of the wall first. Then work outwards from the centre, pulling the fabric taut each time before inserting a staple. Make sure that the bottom staples are in line with the top staples so any pattern does not look pulled out of line.

6 Cut ribbon to roughly the right length. Apply fabric glue according to the maker's instructions and fix the ribbon neatly to the fabric. It should cover the edge of the fabric and the staples. Repeat at the bottom, covering the staples and the edge of the fabric as before.

Finished effect

The fabric panel adds a feeling of warmth, ideal for a bedroom. A patterned fabric such as this might be overwhelming used on the whole wall but adds a pleasing contrast to the plain paintwork above.

Découpage

THE ART OF DECOUPAGE was traditionally designed for decorating screens, trays, and small items of furniture rather than walls, and became a favourite pastime for Victorian ladies. Lots of small pictures were carefully cut out, applied in intricate designs, and given a coat of protective varnish. Découpage on walls is somewhat different and needs larger, more dramatic images. I prefer to break away from the somewhat claustrophobic Victorian style and use découpage in ways that are fun and entertaining. Stick maps on the walls of a hall or cover a kitchen with menus from favourite restaurants. Let your imagination take over.

Découpage does not have to cover a wall. You can use just a few pictures to create an attractive border or a frame for a door. Wrapping paper, greetings cards, and old magazines are all good sources of images.

Découpage border
Beautiful photographs of perfect specimens of fruit make an appealing découpage border for a kitchen. Simple though the idea is, the images must be carefully placed to achieve a good result.

Applying découpage

Only the simplest of equipment is needed. You cut the images out, arrange a design, then tack them to the wall. Taking each item in turn, you draw round the picture to give you a positioning guide, paste the back, and then put it in place on the wall.

Sharp paper scissors

Blu-tack

Adhesive

Palette knife for spreading adhesive

Selection of images

1 Choose the pictures you are going to use for your design. Cut them all out as neatly as you can with a pair of sharp scissors.

2 Put all your pictures on a table and move them around until you have a design that you are happy with and which suits the space that you wish to cover.

3 Tack all the pictures to the wall with Blu-tack, following your final design. Then draw lightly round one of the images with a pencil (see inset) and remove it.

4 Apply adhesive to the back of the picture with a palette knife or spatula. Make sure that the adhesive is spread right to the edges of the picture so that it sticks to the wall properly.

5 Place the pasted picture on the wall, positioning it carefully within the pencil outline. Any pencil marks that show can be rubbed out later. Repeat Steps 3–5 to fix all the other images.

Finished effect

Once all the images are applied, apply several coats of varnish (see p. 73) to protect them and stop them from peeling at the edges. Use flat, satin, or gloss varnish as you prefer. A simple example of the technique, this is a quick way of cheering up plain walls in a child's room.

VARIATION

Découpage can be applied all over a wall with all the images overlapping. Here, old maps have been used to cover a wall, with added butterflies providing a frivolous note.

Glossary

Architrave
The moulding that surrounds a door, arch, or window.

Badger brush
A delicate soft brush made of badger hair, used for softening glaze work.

Bronze powder
A metallic powder available in several shades, this can be used to mix metallic paint and is an excellent substitute for gold leaf.

Button polish
Used in french polishing, button polish is also useful as a bonding agent in metallic paint.

Colourwashing
A simple but effective paint effect with a translucent finish. Acrylic glaze is applied over a base coat of vinyl silk/satin latex and brushed out with large sweeping brush strokes.

Cornice
A moulding that runs round the ceiling at the top of a wall.

Dado
A moulding that runs round the wall at the approximate height of the back of an upright chair.

Découpage
The technique of covering a surface with a collection of cut-out paper images. The images are carefully cut out, stuck down, and varnished.

Distressing
A technique for making a surface such as a door or skirting/baseboard look naturally aged. The surface is painted with quick drying/acrylic latex eggshell and then glazed. The glaze is then lifted with steel wool.

Dragging
A paint effect achieved by dragging a glazed wall with a fine-bristled dragging brush to produce fine, horizontal stripes.

Faux finishes
Finishes that imitate another material such as wood, tortoiseshell, or marble.

Flogger
Long hogshair brush used for coarser finishes.

Frottage
The process of gently pressing newspaper onto wet glaze and removing it quickly to reveal an organic stone or cork-like finish.

Glaze
A translucent mixture of acrylic glaze, water, and pigment colours used for paint effects.

Glider
A finely made soft bristle brush, originally designed for applying varnish but also useful for small areas of dragging and other effects.

Grouting
Fine plaster for filling the spaces between tiles or stone blocks. On trompe l'oeil blocks, grouting can be imitated with paint, usually grey, applied with an artist's brush.

Malachite
A green mineral. An extremely decorative faux finish imitates malachite. Glaze is applied and worked with a piece of thin card into malachite-like patterns.

Marbling
The process of imitating marble. Acrylic glazes are applied over a base of vinyl silk/satin latex and softened with ragging, a feather, and a badger brush.

Masking
A technique used to create a straight painted or stippled line. The masking tape is applied either side of the intended line. The paint is applied between the tape and the tape removed.

Matt emulsion/latex
A flat, water-based paint suitable for use on walls and ceilings.

Methylated spirits
An alcohol-based solvent used for cleaning brushes, mixing metallic paint, and other processes.

Mottler
A small brush without a handle, used for woodgraining.

Moulding
Ornamental and continuous lines of grooving or projections. Dado rails, architraves, picture rails, cornices, and skirting/baseboards are almost always moulded.

Mutton cloth
Cotton woven cloth used for ragging, cleaning brushes, wiping off paint, and many other purposes.

Oil eggshell
An oil-based, durable paint with a satin finish, ideal for woodwork.

Picture rail
Horizontal moulding originally designed for hanging pictures. In an average-sized room, it is usually about 43cm (17in) from the cornice. The gap between the two increases in a taller room.

Porphyry flick
A faux finish, also known as flyspecking, in which small dots of coloured glaze are flicked from a 2.5cm (1in) brush onto a previously glazed surface. The finish imitates a very hard variegated rock called porphyry.

Quick-drying/acrylic latex eggshell
Water-based paint with a silky sheen, this is suitable for woodwork and as a base for acrylic glaze on woodwork. In the United States, the acrylic eggshell is of a higher quality than in Europe.

Skirting/baseboard
Narrow board that runs round the base of walls.

Stencilling
The technique of producing images or patterns with stencils. The intended design is traced onto the stencil paper and cut out with a craft knife. The stencil is then securely held onto the wall and various colours are punched through the cut-out holes with a suitable stencilling or stippling brush.

Stippling
An effect applied to glaze for broken colour work. Box-like square bristle brushes are used to achieve this effect. Once the wet glaze is applied to the wall, it is vigorously and systematically punched with the stippling brush, creating millions of tiny dots.

Tongue and groove
Two boards that are slotted into each other. The projecting tongue of one is slotted into the groove of the other. Tongue and groove boarding can be used to cover walls.

Tortoiseshell
A faux finish that imitates the shell of a tortoise. The area is prepared with vinyl silk/satin latex and glazed and daubs of darker, more concentrated glaze added. These are softened with a badger brush to create a mottled effect.

Trompe l'oeil
The art of deceiving the eye by making a flat painted area look like a three-dimensional image with painted shadow lines.

Varnish
A protective resinous solution produced in non-yellowing, water-based form. Varnish is available in three levels of sheen – flat, satin, and gloss.

Vinyl silk/satin latex
A water-based emulsion with a silky sheen, suitable for use on walls and as a base for acrylic glazes.

Woodgraining
The technique of making a cheap wooden door, or other wooden surface, look as if it is made of mahogany, oak, or other expensive wood. The surface is glazed and appropriate grain markings are applied with a mottler and a flogging brush.

Index

INDEX OF TECHNIQUES

The following special techniques are used in the Style Directory

Colourwashing Colourwashed rough plaster pp. 30–31; Strong colourwash pp. 38–39; Colourwashed wall with blue woodwork pp. 46–47; Sea-green colourwash and plastic bagging pp. 50–51

Découpage Découpage maps pp. 24–25; Fruit découpage on green pp. 32–33

Distressing Marbled blocks p. 22; Stone blocks and distressed wood pp. 34–35

Dragging Stone blocks and distressed wood pp. 34–35; Dragged trompe l'oeil panels pp. 46–47; Yellow dragging in two tones p. 50; Leaf stencil pp. 50–51; Flower border stencil on ragged wall pp. 62–63

Fabric Green baize wall with ribbon dado p. 42; Fabric panel pp. 62–63

Foam roller stripes Foam roller stripes pp. 60–61

Frottage Stone blocks and distressed wood pp. 34–35; Frottage wall and door p. 46; Yellow frottage p. 60

Malachite Geometric stencil and malachite p. 38

Marbling Marbled blocks p. 22

Plastic bagging Sea-green colourwash and plastic bagging pp. 50–51

Porphyry flick Subtle porphyry flick p. 48

Ragging Metallic stencils on ragged wall pp. 38–39; Red ragged wall with gold pp. 40–41; Red ragging and black woodwork pp. 48–49; Leaf stencil pp. 50–51; Damask stencil p. 62; Flower border stencil on ragged wall pp. 62–63

Rough plaster Colourwashed rough plaster p. 30

Stencilling Key stencil pp. 22–23; Black stencil on red p. 26; Bull stencil on green pp. 26–27; Melon and cherry stencil pp. 34–35; Geometric stencil and malachite p. 38; Metallic stencils on ragged wall pp. 38–39; Black and gold stencilled squares pp. 42–43; Leaf stencil pp. 50–51; Crab and fish stencil pp. 56–57; Giraffe stencil pp. 60–61; Damask stencil p. 62; Flower border stencil on ragged wall pp. 62–63

Stippling Blue stipple pp. 40–41

Tartan Tartan p. 40

Tiling Blue tiles on white emulsion pp. 30–31; Pale blue walls with blue tiles pp. 32–33; Lime wallpaper and white tiles p. 54

Tortoiseshell Green walls with tortoiseshell band pp. 54–55

Trompe l'oeil Trompe l'oeil umbrella stand p. 24; Dragged trompe l'oeil panels pp. 46–47; Trompe l'oeil leaves pp. 54–55

Wallpaper Black and white urn wallpaper pp. 26–27; Primitive animal wallpaper pp. 30–31; Tree wallpaper pp. 42–43; Chinese wallpaper pp. 48–49; Lime wallpaper and white tiles p. 54; Deep blue wallpaper p. 56

Wide paint-effect stripes Wide stripes and woodgrained door pp. 22–23; Pale wide stripes pp. 24–25

Wide stripes Yellow and white wide stripes p. 32; Wavy stripes pp. 56–57

Woodgraining Wide stripes and woodgrained door pp. 22–23

Credits

Author's acknowledgements

My very big thanks to Lucinda Symons for her zest with the photography, to Yuk Ping Kwan for assisting, and to Sarah Davies for her panache in creating rope from string. Thanks, too, to Steve Gott for lateral thinking and especially to Jinny Johnson, my editor, for her constant steering and reassurance. Last, but not least, I'd like to thank Collins and Brown, and Jessica Prendergast, my long-suffering, long-fingered hand model.

Special thanks, too, to the following for their helpful advice on professional matters:

Patrick Baty from Papers and Paints, London

Simon Rosenblum from Janovic Plaza, New York

Toby Nuttall, decorative painter based in New York

Kate Bologna, decorative painter based in London

Georgina Markes, my ex-decorative painting partner

Annie Sloan, friend and supporter for 20 years

Mary Gilliatt, friend and inspirer

Equipment came from the following sources:

C. P. Hart, 103 Regents Park Road, London NW1 8UR (bathroom basin and taps); Designers Guild, 277 King's Road, London SW3 5EN (wallpaper); Fired Earth, 102 Portland Road, London W11 4LX (tiles); Heal's, 196 Tottenham Court Road, London W1P 9LP (wrapping paper); Ian Mankin, 109 Regents Park Road, London NW18UR (fabric); Leyland Paints, 361–365 Kensington High Street, London W14 8QY (paint kettles); Newsons, 491 Battersea Park Road, London SW11 4LR (wooden dado rails, skirting/baseboards, etc); Osborne & Little, 304 King's Road, London SW3 5UH (wallpaper); Papers & Paints, 4 Park Walk, London SW10 OAD (decorating materials and specialist paints and brushes); Peter Jones, Sloane Square, London SW1 8EL (tiles, ribbon, and fabric); Timney Fowler, 388 King's Road, London SW3 5UZ (wallpaper)

Photography

Style panels (except for those listed below) and step-by-step photography by Lucinda Symons.
The author and publishers also wish to thank the following photographers and organizations for their kind permission to reproduce the photographs listed:

7 Michael Crockett; 8 Laura Jeannes/Camera Press, London; 11 Paul Ryan/International Interiors/Peter Wentz Farmstead; 12 Michael Brockway/Robert Harding Picture Library; 13 above left, Fritz von der Schulenburg (designer: Mimmi O'Connell/Peter Farlow); 13 below left, Steven Hawkins/Elizabeth Whiting & Associates; 14 above, Fritz von der Schulenburg (designer: Paula Navone); 15 below Paul Grootes/VT Wonen; 16 above, Alan Weintraub (designer: Robin Nelson) Arcaid; 17 above, Richard Bryant/Arcaid; 20 Fritz von der Schulenburg (designer: Monica Apponyi); 21 above, Fritz von der Schulenburg (courtesy of the Al Fayed Archive); 21 below James Merrell/Woman's Journal/Robert Harding Syndication; 25 left, Michael Crockett; 28 Dennis Stone/Elizabeth Whiting & Associates; 29 Fritz von der Schulenburg (designer: Richard Hudson); 35 left, Michael Crockett; 36 James Merrell/Options/Robert Harding Syndication; 37 Dennis Stone/Elizabeth Whiting & Associates; 41 left, Michael Crockett; 43 left, Michael Crockett; 44 Joanne Cowie/Country Homes & Interiors/Robert Harding Syndication; 45 above, Fritz von der Schulenburg (designer: Mimmi O'Connell /Juliette Mole); 45 below, Elizabeth Whiting & Associates; 52 Fritz von der Schulenburg (designer: Paula Navone); 53 above, Graham Rae/Woman's Journal/Robert Harding Syndication; 53 below, Jon Bouchier/Elizabeth Whiting & Associates; 58 Paul Ryan/International Interiors (designers: John and Myra Frost); 59 above, Paul Ryan/International Interiors (designers: John Saladino); 59 below, Marianne Haas/Michel Biehn's House, Provence/Elle Decoration. 61 right, Michael Crockett.